WHAT YOU NEED TO KNOW ABOUT THE CHURCH

12 LESSONS THAT CAN CHANGE YOUR LIFE

MAX ANDERS

AUTHOR OF *30 DAYS TO UNDERSTANDING THE BIBLE*

THOMAS NELSON
Since 1798

NASHVILLE DALLAS MEXICO CITY RIO DE JANEIRO

Library of Congress Cataloging-in-Publication Data

Anders, Max E., 1947–

What You Need to Know About The Church/Max Anders.

Includes bibliographical references.

ISBN 978-1-4185-4856-8 (pbk.)

1. Church—Study and teaching.   I. Title.   II. Series.

BV600.2.A49 1997

262—dc20

97–5898

CIP

CONTENTS

INTRODUCTION TO THE
WHAT YOU NEED TO KNOW SERIES

You hold in your hands a tool with enormous potential—the ability to help ground you, and a whole new generation of other Christians, in the basics of the Christian faith.

I believe the times call for just this tool. We face a serious crisis in the church today . . . namely, a generation of Christians who know the truth but who do not live it. An even greater challenge is coming straight at us, however: a coming generation of Christians who may not even know the truth!

Many Christian leaders agree that today's evangelical church urgently needs a tool flexible enough to be used by a wide variety of churches to ground current and future generations of Christians in the basics of Scripture and historic Christianity.

This guide, and the whole series from which it comes—the *What You Need to Know* series—can be used by individuals or groups for just that reason.

Here are five other reasons why we believe you will enjoy using this guide:

1. It is easy to read.

You don't want to wade through complicated technical jargon to try to stumble on the important truths you are looking for. This series puts biblical truth right out in the open. It is written in a warm and friendly style, with even a smattering of humor here and there. See if you don't think it is different from anything you have ever read before.

2. It is easy to teach.

You don't want to spend ten hours preparing for Sunday school, small group, or discipleship lessons. On the other hand, you don't want watered-down material that insults your group's intellect. There is real meat in these pages, but it is presented in a way that is easy to teach. It follows a question-and-answer format that can be used to cover the material, along with discussion questions at the end of each chapter that make it easy to get group interaction going.

3. It is thoroughly biblical.

You believe the Bible, and don't want to use anything that isn't thoroughly biblical. This series has been written and reviewed by a team of well-educated, personally committed Christians who have a high view of Scripture, and great care has been taken to reflect what the Bible teaches. If the Bible is unambiguous on a subject, such as the resurrection of Christ, then that subject is presented unambiguously.

4. It respectfully presents differing evangelical positions.

You don't want anyone forcing conclusions on you that you don't agree with. There are many subjects in the Bible on which there is more than one responsible position. When that is the case, this series presents those positions with respect, accuracy, and fairness. In fact, to make sure, a team of evaluators from various evangelical perspectives has reviewed each of the volumes in this series.

5. It lets you follow up with your own convictions and distinctives on a given issue.

You may have convictions on an issue that you want to communicate to the people to whom you are ministering. These books give you that flexibility. After presenting the various responsible positions that may be held on a given subject, you will then find it easy to identify and expand upon your view, or the view of your church.

We send this study guide to you with the prayer that God may use it to help strengthen His church for her work in these days.

HOW TO TEACH THIS BOOK

The books in this series are written so that they can be used as a thirteen-week curriculum, ideal for Sunday school classes or other small group meetings. You will notice that there are only twelve chapters—to allow for a session when you may want to do something else. Every quarter seems to call for at least one different type of session, because of holidays, summer vacation, or other special events. If you use all twelve chapters, and still have a session left in the quarter, have a fellowship meeting with refreshments, and use the time to get to know others better. Or use the session to invite newcomers in hopes they will continue with the course.

All ten books in the series together form a "Basic Knowledge Curriculum" for Christians. Certainly, Christians would eventually want to know more than is in these books, but they should not know less. Therefore, the series is excellent for seekers, for new Christians, and for Christians who may not have a solid foundation of biblical education. It is also a good series for those whose biblical education has been spotty.

Of course, the books can also be used in small groups and discipleship groups. If you are studying the book by yourself, you can simply read the chapters and go through the material at the end. If you are using the books to teach others, you might find the following guidelines helpful:

Teaching Outline

1. Begin the session with prayer.

2. Consider having a quiz at the beginning of each meeting over the self-test from the chapter to be studied for that day. The quiz can be optional, or the group may want everyone to commit to it, depending on the setting in which the material is taught. In a small discipleship group or one-on-one, it might be required. In a larger Sunday school class, it might need to be optional.

3. At the beginning of the session, summarize the material. You may want to have class members be prepared to summarize the material. You might want to bring in information that was not covered in the book. There might be some in the class who have not read the material, and this will help catch them up with those who did. Even for those who did read it, a summary will refresh their minds and get everyone into a common mind-set. It may also generate questions and discussion.

4. Discuss the material at the end of the chapters as time permits. Use whatever you think best fits the group.

5. Have a special time for questions and answers, or encourage questions during the course of discussion. If you are asked a question you can't answer (it happens to all of us), just say you don't know, but that you will find out. Then, the following week, you can open the question-and-answer time, or perhaps the discussion time, with the answer to the question from last week.

6. Close with prayer.

You may have other things you would like to incorporate, and flexibility is the key to success. These suggestions are given only to guide, not to dictate. Prayerfully choose a plan suited to your circumstances.

1

WHAT IS THE CHURCH?

A Christian church is a body or collection of persons, voluntarily associated together, professing to believe what Christ teaches, to do what Christ enjoins, to imitate His example, cherish His spirit, and make known His gospel to others.
—R. F. Sample

I was born in the little village of Inwood, Indiana. It is about a half hour south of the golden dome of the University of Notre Dame in South Bend, but you'll be lucky if you find it on a map. There were only about thirty homes, sheltering perhaps one hundred people, with a gas station, a small grocery store, a post office, a grain elevator, an elementary school, and one church. We lived just a block from the church, which was a large, stone-block building with stained-glass windows, solid mahogany pews and altar, and many friendly people, all of whom lived within walking distance or a short drive from the church. Sunday school began at 9:00 A.M., and at 8:55 A.M. a bell in the steeple began ringing, calling all the townspeople. Our family emerged from our house like little ducks headed toward the pond, and a few minutes later, we were in our place in church.

My earliest memories of church were warm and comforting. My family was there—not just immediate family, but aunts, uncles, cousins, and grandmother. I remember all these and other people singing songs that everyone knew by heart, and before long, even I knew some of them. Occasionally the hymns would have an echo as part of the song. Sopranos, tenors, and basses would sing the stanza, and then the melody line would be echoed by the altos. Most of the altos were timid souls, but not my grandmother. Annabell Anders, matriarch of the Inwood Methodist Church, belted out the echo as though the songwriter had written it especially for her. Years later, after she had died, I was in the church again, and another alto sang the echo. I was offended! Who was this interloper singing my grandmother's part?

I attended church every Sunday until I was tall enough to look my mother in the eye. My three older sisters had left home by then, and my two older brothers had

9

quit going, so I did too. I didn't know why I quit. I was just going along with what everyone else seemed to be doing. Plus, my increasingly late Saturday nights made early Sunday mornings more and more difficult.

I became a Christian in college, then went away to seminary, got married, and entered the ministry. I have only been back a few times since then, but my memories of the big stone church are good ones.

Today, the church looks largely unchanged. They built it well. The stone blocks haven't aged. The stained-glass windows are as colorful as ever. The wooden pews are as beautiful and uncomfortable as ever. And friendly folk who have known each other for a lifetime still find their way into the pews each Sunday.

IN THIS CHAPTER WE LEARN THAT . . .

1. The universal church is made up of all true Christians everywhere, past, present, and future.

2. The universal church is pictured in Scripture by a body, a building, and a bride.

3. A local church is a group of believers who agree together to pursue the ideals of the universal church.

From my earliest days, if you were to ask me what the church is, a large, gray stone-block building would flash into my mind. That image would be followed by memories of red and blue light from the stained-glass windows falling across the hardwood floors, giving a soft glow to the interior. The rich wood tones of the pews, pulpit, and altar rail finish the timeless look of it all. That was the church, in my mind.

It came as a bit of a surprise to me when I learned many years later that, biblically speaking, that was *not* the church. The church was not a building. The church was people. We don't *go* to church. We *are* the church. In fact, there are Christian groups who don't call their building a church. They call the building a "meeting house." They call the *people* the church. In the truest sense, they are right.

It is difficult to get an accurate concept of and appreciation for the church. It is like many things in life. It is greater than it initially seems. I remember when I saw the Washington Monument for the first time. I took it for granted. It is a tall, thin, white stone pillar sticking way up above the rest of the city, the height of a fifty-story building. Building that memorial so that it wouldn't fall over in a stiff wind was a stunning achievement. If you have ever tried to stack children's blocks and had them fall over, you can imagine how difficult it would be to build the Washington Monument. Had I built it, it would be lying on its side now.

WHY I NEED TO KNOW THIS

The church in the United States is in a very weakened condition. Many Christians have lost respect for the church because of human failure. Rather than turning our backs on the church because of past human failures, we need to commit ourselves to helping the church fulfill its proper role. Unless we see the church as God sees it, we will be contributing to the problems of Christianity, rather than helping solve them.

Or, in another example, take Mount Rushmore. Each of the presidential faces on that staggering monument is the size of a six-story building. Yet they really look like Washington, Jefferson, Lincoln, and Teddy Roosevelt. If you have ever had any trouble getting a sand castle to look the way you wanted, imagine the difficulty of blasting a granite mountain with dynamite and having it turn out to look like real people!

Finally, if you have ever had trouble closing your eyes and touching the first fingers of both hands out in front of you, imagine how difficult it was when the French and British dug a tunnel under the English Channel, each country starting from its own shore, and meeting in the middle under the water. Left to me, they would have passed each other in the rock and would still be digging a tunnel around the world, wondering where the other guy was.

Monumental human achievements such as these are easy to take for granted until we try to figure out how we would do them if they were our responsibility. Suddenly we realize what amazing feats they are.

The church, by comparison, is a tremendous *divine* achievement. It is also easy to take the church for granted, thinking less of it than we ought to because of our lack of understanding. The church is a big deal to God, and we must try to expand our understanding and appreciation of it until it is a big deal to us.

WHAT IS THE UNIVERSAL CHURCH?

The universal church is made up of all true Christians everywhere, past, present, and future.

In order to gain a fuller understanding of the universal church we will look at some of the things that the universal church is, and some of the things it is not.

The Church Is Not a Building.

People can become understandably confused about what the church is. Like me, some people are misled into assuming that the church is a building or an organization, rather than a collection of people. In the original language of the New Testament, however, the Greek word for "church" helps us clarify our understanding. *Ekklesia*, translated "church," means an assembly, or a group called together for a meeting. *Ek* means "out from" (like exit), and *kaleo* means "called." Together, the two words mean "called out" and assembled together. The same word would be used whether or not the meeting was a religious one.

For instance, in Acts 19, the town clerk of the city of Ephesus was concerned that a riot was going to break out over the apostle Paul's preaching. He urged his fellow citizens, who had gathered to discuss the matter, to remain calm and file legal charges against Paul, rather than resort to violence. "And when he had said these things, he dismissed the assembly" (v. 41). The word "assembly" is *ekklesia*.

The word later came to be used of Christians, people who had been called together spiritually to follow Jesus. The word as used in the New Testament usually refers to a local congregation of Christians. But it also refers to the universal church, the spiritual gathering together of all true Christians: "[God] put all things under His [Christ's] feet, and gave Him to be head over all things to the church (*ekklesia*), which is His body" (Ephesians 1:22–23). In the Bible, the church never means a building where people meet, but rather refers to the people themselves.

The Church Is People.

The people who are part of the universal church are those who have received Jesus Christ as their personal Savior. Earthly membership in a local congregation, however, is no guarantee of being a part of the spiritual universal church. Someone has said that going into a church building doesn't make you a Christian any more than going into a garage makes you a car, or going into a barn makes you a cow. It is not what happens on the outside that matters, but what happens on the inside.

Even in the Old Testament, merely being born into the nation of Israel did not make a person one of God's people, spiritually. The apostle Paul wrote,

> A man is not a Jew if he is only one outwardly, nor is circumcision merely outward and physical. No, a man is a Jew if he is one inwardly; and circumcision is circumcision of the heart, by the Spirit, not by the written code. (Romans 2:28–29 NIV)

The same is true of Christians. Using similar words, a person is not a Christian if he/she is one merely outwardly. No, a person is a Christian if he is one inwardly;

and becoming a member of the universal church is the result of what has happened in the heart, not of getting one's name on the membership register of a local church.

The Church Is a Divine Creation.

The church was first mentioned by Jesus when He said, "You are Peter, and on this rock I will build My church, and the gates of Hades [hell] shall not prevail against it" (Matthew 16:18). There is some question as to what He meant by that statement. What is the rock upon which Jesus will build His church? The Roman Catholic position is that the rock refers to Peter. Their understanding is that Peter was the first pope, and all other popes over the church are in direct succession to Peter's office and authority.

However, the traditional Protestant interpretations differ, based on the context of the statement and Jesus' choice of words concerning the "rock":

When Jesus came into the region of Caesarea Philippi, He asked His disciples, saying, "Who do men say that I, the Son of Man, am?"

So they said, "Some say John the Baptist, some Elijah, and others Jeremiah or one of the prophets."

He said to them, "But who do you say that I am?"

Simon Peter answered and said, "You are the Christ, the Son of the living God."

Jesus answered and said to him, "Blessed are you, Simon Bar-Jonah, for flesh and blood has not revealed this to you, but My Father who is in heaven.

"And I also say to you that you are Peter, and on this rock I will build My church, and the gates of Hades shall not prevail against it." (Matthew 16:13–18)

In this context of Peter's having just declared Jesus to be the Christ, the Son of God, the rock could be Christ Himself. Also, the Greek word for "Peter" is *petros* and means a stone or boulder. But the Greek word for the "rock" on which Jesus says He will build His church is *petra,* which means a mass of rock, not a detached stone or boulder that might be thrown. Or, the context could mean that the *confession* of Jesus' being the Christ could be that rock upon which Jesus would build His church. Either one would be consistent with Scripture and history.

> The church is a tremendous *divine* achievement.

There are differences of opinion as to when the church actually began. Some believe it began when God began redeeming His people. Many people connect it to the New Testament and Jesus' ministry in particular. In Matthew 16:18, Jesus seems to suggest that His church was still in the future ("I *will* build My church"). The word for church is used again in Matthew 18:17, but since the word can refer to any assembly of people, and since there were no Christian assemblies yet, it could easily have been referring to the Jewish assembly, or synagogue.

The next use of the word for church is found in Acts 2:47, shortly after the day of Pentecost, and subsequent uses of the word clearly refer to the church. Therefore, there is strong support for concluding that the church came into existence in early Acts, probably on the day of Pentecost in Acts 2. This reinforces the concept of the church being "people," since the emphasis in early Acts is on people beginning to believe in Jesus.

Bible students are also divided as to when the church will cease, but we can say, generally speaking, that when the events of history culminate, the church will also culminate. History as we know it will end and eternity will begin. At some point during those dramatic events, the universal church will be complete.

HOW IS THE UNIVERSAL CHURCH PICTURED IN SCRIPTURE?

The universal church is pictured in Scripture as a body, a building, and a bride.

The Bible gives a number of word pictures of the church, images that help us understand more of the nature of the universal church.

A Body

Doctors tell us that, because of the continuous dying and replacing of cells in our body, we get a new body every seven years. If that is the case, in my first three bodies, each new one was better than the last. However, I have gotten a number of bodies since I was twenty-one, and in those cases, each one has been worse than the last! I cringe to imagine the next three. Even with the limitations of our earthly body, however, we can imagine a heavenly body—a body without defect—and this helps us to understand more fully what the church is.

The apostle Paul's favorite picture for the church was the body. It is a word picture communicating the fact that Christians on earth are the hands, feet, and tongue of Christ, that we are to labor, travel, and speak what Christ would if He were in our shoes. Jesus is the head of the body, and each of us makes up our part of His spiritual body on earth. We each have different functions, different abilities, different callings, and different locations. Romans 12:4–5 reads, "Just as each of us has one body with many members, and these members do not all have the same function, so in Christ we who are many form one body, and each member belongs to all the others" (NIV).

We do not become the body when we agree to work together in harmony. We are automatically the body, regardless of whether or not we decide to work together in harmony. The question is only whether we will be a healthy body or an unhealthy one. We are not a member of the body when we decide to join a local church. If we are Christians, we are already members of the body. We are not added to the body or subtracted from the body by our choice. If we belong to Christ, we are members, and we belong to each other because we are all in Christ.

If Christians ever came to understand and appreciate that truth, it would make us more tolerant of those who are different and more aware of our need for others with diverse abilities. Just as a human body could not function if all its members were the same, so the body of Christ could not function if we were all the same.

A Building

One of the grandest buildings in Washington, D.C., is the National Cathedral. It is a huge stone cathedral with stunning architectural lines, magnificent stained-glass windows, a lovely altar, and beautiful grounds. When I visited it the first time many years ago, they had been working on it for many years. It was open to the public, but parts of it were still not finished. We went out to a construction area where we saw stone carvers, some of the last such craftsmen in the world, still chipping away at ornate blocks of granite. Today, the cathedral is still not complete. It will be complete one day, but the task is so huge that the construction life of the cathedral exceeds the life of anyone working on it.

So it is with the universal church. A second picture of the church is that of a spiritual building. The apostle Paul wrote in Ephesians, "You are . . . of the household of God, having been built on the foundation of the apostles and prophets, Jesus Christ Himself being the chief cornerstone,

> The church is a body of many valuable members, a building that grows, and a bride who will be honored by her heavenly Groom!

in whom the whole building, being fitted together, grows into a holy temple in the Lord, in whom you also are being built together for a dwelling place of God in the Spirit" (2:19–22).

We can imagine, in our mind's eye, that huge cathedral having a name on each of the stones. Figuratively speaking, one of those stones is Bill, one is Susan, one is James, one is Katherine, and—*glory to God*—one is Max!

There are three truths about the church that are presented in this passage, as well as a companion passage in 1 Corinthians 3:10–17. First, the church has an eternal foundation of the apostles and prophets, the cornerstone of which is Jesus Christ. The foundation is secure. It cannot be removed or replaced. It ensures that the building that rests on it will be secure.

Second, the building is always growing, always being added to. There is a master plan. All the stones that will eventually make up this great human superstructure were planned before the building was ever begun. And, if you are a Christian, you are one of the stones.

Third, the building is the dwelling place of God in the Spirit. He fills the building with His presence and conveys on it infinite value with His blessing.

A Bride

We have all been to weddings, and what has been the focal point of every one of them? The bride. Everything in the entire service centers around the bride, highlights the bride, honors the bride. The minister is in place, the groom and his attendants stand at the front, ladies come down the aisle, flower girls drop rose petals, heightening the anticipation for the crowning moment: the appearance of the bride. The music swells, everyone's head turns, and the bride, beaming, appears at the back. All stand. She walks down on the arm of her father and the entire gathering turns slowly with her passing. Grandmothers weep quietly, mothers blubber openly, fathers bite lips—all for the bride.

Then the vows are given, and the bride is united to the groom. The two become one.

That is the destiny of Christians. Someday in heaven we will be honored as no bride on earth has ever been honored. To think that Jesus would honor us! It is we who should honor Him, and yet, a ceremony confirming His marriage to us is conducted in heaven. The apostle John wrote, "Hallelujah! For the Lord our God, the Almighty, reigns. Let us rejoice and be glad and give the glory to Him, for the marriage of the Lamb has come and His bride has made herself ready.... Blessed are those who are invited to the marriage supper of the Lamb" (Revelation 19:6–7, 9 NASB).

Are these not amazing pictures? You are the body of Christ. You are the temple of God in the Spirit. You are the bride of Christ. As the body, you have a task, you are gifted. As a building, you belong, you are possessed and indwelt by the living God, you reflect His glory. As a bride, you are honored, you are owned, you are glorified. By whom? Of all persons, by Jesus!

Is this not too much to take in? It is Cinderella, all over again. A handsome prince sees a peasant girl who is in bondage to evil. The prince subdues the power of evil, marries Cinderella, and takes her to his castle to live happily ever after. We are all

Cinderella. No matter how hard this life on earth might be for you, take hope. One day, you will live in a palace with the King of heaven.

The Church Has Common Life.

These different word pictures of the church reveal a life held in common and continue to expand the idea that the emphasis of Scripture regarding the church is on "people." We have observed in another volume in this series (*What You Need to Know about the Holy Spirit*) that each person in the church is given a spiritual gift. He or she is to use that gift in serving the other people in the church, and to build one another up. As the members of the church each use their spiritual gift for the benefit of the other Christians, all are able to grow to spiritual maturity in Christ (Ephesians 4:11–16; 1 Peter 4:10).

In addition to this mutual ministry, a number of passages in Scripture encourage us to live in harmony, unity, and symbiosis with one another. The list of "one anothers" is impressive when we consider what it would really be like to live among people who did these things for one another:

- Be kindly affectionate to one another . . . , giving preference to one another, Romans 12:10.
- Be of the same mind toward one another, Romans 12:16.
- Let us not judge one another, Romans 14:13.
- Build up one another, Romans 14:19 (NASB).
- Be of the same mind with one another, Romans 15:5 (NASB).
- Accept one another, Romans 15:7 (NIV).
- Admonish one another, Romans 15:14.
- Have the same care for one another, 1 Corinthians 12:25.
- Serve one another, Galatians 5:13.
- Show tolerance to one another in love, Ephesians 4:2 (NASB).
- Be kind to one another, tenderhearted, forgiving one another, Ephesians 4:32.
- Be subject to one another, Ephesians 5:21 (NASB).
- Regard one another as more important, Philippians 2:3 (NASB).
- Bear with one another, and forgive one another, Colossians 3:13.
- Comfort one another, 1 Thessalonians 4:18.
- Encourage one another, and build up one another, 1 Thessalonians 5:11 (NASB).
- Live in peace with one another, 1 Thessalonians 5:13 (NASB).
- Seek after that which is good for one another, 1 Thessalonians 5:15 (NASB).
- But encourage one another, Hebrews 3:13 (NASB).

- Confess your sins to one another, and pray for one another, James 5:16 (NASB).
- Be hospitable to one another, 1 Peter 4:9.
- Serve one another, 1 Peter 4:10 (NRSV).
- Clothe yourselves with humility toward one another, 1 Peter 5:5 (NASB).
- Love one another, 1 John 3:11.

These are some of the ideals of the universal church. What a bit of heaven on earth would be created if we were to be part of a local congregation such as this—giving and receiving in full measure, part of a larger whole, loving and being loved. What a testimony it would be to a watching world. What a glory it would be to God. We cannot control how others act, but as much as it lies within us, we can try to do our part.

WHAT IS THE LOCAL CHURCH?

A local church is a group of believers who agree together to pursue the ideals of the universal church.

While the universal church is clearly presented in Scripture, the most frequent use of the word *church* refers to specific local congregations who have agreed together to pursue the ideals of the universal church. To do that, the people must fulfill several functions and responsibilities. We see in the New Testament several things that must be true of the local church for it to actually be a church.

A Local Church Meets Regularly.

If a group of people are actually to be a church, they must gather regularly for worship. Hebrews 10:24–25 says, "And let us consider one another in order to stir up love and good works, not forsaking the assembling of ourselves together, as is the manner of some." Worship of God is certainly the central priority of any local church. From the examples of worship we see in the Bible, we may conclude that corporate worship involves the preaching of the Word, prayer, music, celebration, and the giving of offerings (2 Chronicles 5—7; Nehemiah 12:27—13:1). From further instructions in the New Testament, we learn that baptism (Matthew 28:19) and communion (1 Corinthians 11:23–26) also must be observed in the local church. In addition, the church is commissioned to take the message of the gospel to the entire unsaved world. Evangelism and making disciples is certainly one of the fundamental responsibilities of the church (Matthew 28:18–20).

A Local Church Has Qualified Leaders.

The apostle Paul made it clear that pastors were key people in the life of a church, necessary to equip the saints for the work of ministry and the spiritual growth of the congregation (Ephesians 4:11–12). In addition, elders are to be selected to give spiritual oversight to the congregation and to shepherd them (1 Timothy 3:1–7). Finally, deacons are to look after the physical needs of the congregation (Acts 6:1–6; 1 Timothy 3:8–13). All these people must meet the qualifications set down in these passages. (This subject will be dealt with more thoroughly in chapters 6 and 7.)

A Local Church Is Organized.

As soon as a church was formed in the Bible, it got organized (Acts 14:21–23; Titus 1:5) so that it could fulfill the responsibilities of a church. In Acts 2:42–47, we see the church worshiping, we see it growing in knowledge of Scripture, we see it fellowshiping and providing mutual encouragement, and we see it having an impact on those around it. These are the tasks of a church, and we see the church organizing, with spiritual leaders, so that the proper functioning of the local church can take place.

One lamentable responsibility of the church is not only to encourage the spiritual maturity of its people, but also to discipline outrageous, public, and steadfastly unrepentant sin (1 Corinthians 5). The purpose of such discipline is to bring about repentance and restoration of the offending person (2 Corinthians 2:5–7).

> By biblical definition, every true church gathers for worship, instruction, and service, under mature leaders authorized to build up and discipline in Christ's name.

Some who hold an informal view of the church suggest that the simplest form of the church is found in Matthew 18:20, "For where two or three are gathered together in My name, I am there in the midst of them." This is too shallow an understanding of the church, however. That verse is dealing with procedures for confronting a sinning brother, not for conducting a church. "Two or three gathered together" might be sufficient for dealing with a sinning brother, or for a time of prayer, or mutual encouragement, or Bible study. But it is not a church. Unless they meet regularly, unless there is spiritually mature leadership, unless there is corporate worship, unless baptism and communion are exercised, unless it is organized for mutual ministry and spiritual growth, unless church discipline is present, and unless there is outreach into the world, it is not a church. (We will look more closely at forms of church government in chapter 9.)

A Local Church Is Not a Country Club.

Some also see the church as something you join for what you can get out of it, the way you join a country club or the Rotary Club. Certainly, the sincere Christian will get something out of a biblical church, but his primary goal is not the same as that for joining a country club. The church is a place to face the truth and respond accordingly. The apostle Paul described the church of the living God as the "pillar and ground [foundation] of the truth" (1 Timothy 3:15). Unless truth undergirds the church and our role in it, it is just a country club.

The church and our society are in a struggle for the truth. Do we know what it is? Do we embrace it? Do we defend it? Do we promote it? It is becoming easier and easier to fudge a little here, get a little fuzzy there, tune into the values of society to make people feel comfortable without fully confronting truth. People will then be more willing to join our churches—not to become a holy nation for the Lord, but to join our country club, if the price isn't too high, and if the show is good enough.

If we do not call people to lives of serious discipleship, we have nothing to justify our existence. We might as well shut the doors and go do something else. We are called to be a witness, and we dare not water down our message for fear of offending people. There is no virtue in needlessly offending people, and many churches have certainly done that. But neither is there any virtue in capitulating to secular values.

A Local Church Is a Covenant Community.

A covenant community is a group of people who have entered into a serious agreement with each other. When we become followers of Christ, we become members of His universal church, and we cannot be fully committed to Christ without also being committed to His church. I do not mean that we must be committed to a so-called church with which we have no shared values. But we must be committed to the ideals of the universal church as seen most clearly in faithful local churches, and our commitment should be to find the best local church we can, join it, and help make it better. Or to help start one if none exists.

> **Belonging to a church is fundamental to the faithful Christian life.**

The church is not a country club, but Christianity is corporate. Many parts make up a whole. We belong to each other; we need each other. We are the community of the redeemed. No church is a social center, or a civic center or an encounter group. It is a new society, created for the salvation of a lost world, for the edification of the redeemed, looking forward to a world to come. Properly, the church lives in this world with its eyes on the next—not neglecting this world, but admitting that it is not our home. The church belongs to God, and we must operate it accordingly.

On the other hand, membership in or commitment to a local congregation is a biblical expectation. The pattern seen in the book of Acts is for each believer to make a public confession of faith in Christ, be baptized, and become part of a local congregation with all the privileges and responsibilities that involves. Unfortunately, it is common today for Christians to drift from church to church, or to attend for a while, then stop, depending on how busy they are otherwise, and how good the show is on Sunday morning. Many have no sense of roots or responsibility.

Yet, *belonging* to a church (whether or not your congregation has actual membership; some churches are so low-key about it that they don't even have membership—I used to pastor one) is fundamental to the faithful Christian life.

> **Too many of us see the church as some puny organization that pesters us for money while giving us inferior performances in return.**

When someone is first converted to Christ and comes into the universal church, a first step of discipleship is commitment to a local church. True, it is sometimes difficult to find a church that you "match" well with. Someone has said that the church is like Noah's ark. The stench on the inside would be unbearable if it weren't for the storm outside. However, imperfect as the local church is (and if it were perfect when you got there, it would no longer be perfect afterward), it is still the vehicle God has chosen to be the primary manifestation of His universal church.

CONCLUSION

We began by saying that the church is a big deal to God, and our task is to expand our understanding of and appreciation for the church until it becomes a big deal to us. I want to conclude by nurturing that goal.

Too many of us have too small a picture of the church. I believe this is an overreaction to the dead orthodoxy and lifeless bureaucracy that characterized liberal churches earlier in the twentieth century. The leadership of the church got out of touch with its membership, and many earnest and zealous Christians left the church, believing that it had become irrelevant.

Many reacted strongly to denominational controls and bureaucratic organization and threw it all off. Many new churches were started that were independent of any outside control. This reaction is understandable. When I became a Christian in the mid-sixties, I was in full support of jettisoning the irrelevant baggage of church structures that were more concerned with their own well-being than they were the true functions of the church.

However, in reacting strongly to the excesses of the past, we created our own excesses of the present. We were left with an inadequate grasp of the importance of the church, inadequate respect for church leadership, the ordinances, and church discipline, a weak realization of the need for organization and structure, and an inadequate appreciation for the authority of the church as the body of Christ. If Jesus is the head of the church, then the church had better find out what Jesus thinks, and do things His way.

Too many of us see the church as some puny organization that pesters us for money while giving us inferior performances in return. It has been so long since we have seen the church act like what it is, that we have lost our collective memory of how we should act.

Yes, we all belong to the church if we belong to Jesus. But we belong by virtue of who we are in Christ. If our membership were dependent on the value of our personal involvement, many of us would be defrocked.

It was the church that bled and died to keep the message of salvation alive. From the time of Jesus until the present, God's children have been tortured, beaten, imprisoned, stoned, sawn in two, slain with the sword, fed to lions, and forced to live as fugitives, all because they would not renounce their belief in Christ, or because they would not stop preaching the Word and sharing their faith.

During the disintegration of communism in the Soviet Union and Eastern Europe during the last days of the twentieth century, it was the church that led the way. Chuck Colson, in his insightful volume on the church, *The Body*, tells the story of the church in Timisoara, Romania. An ugly building across the main square houses the Hungarian Reformed Church. On the outside wall of the church hangs a plaque that declares simply, "Here began the revolution that felled a dictator."

Not long after the Soviets overran Romania in August 1944, Nicolae Ceausescu became dictator and imposed on his country an oppressive regime that rivals the worst ever seen. While his people lived in squalor and starved, Ceausescu lived in shameless opulence. Though his regime oppressed everyone, he was particularly repressive toward Christianity. Because many priests of the Romanian Orthodox Church decided that compromise was a reasonable price to pay for existence,

Ceausescu was able to gain control of the church. Catholics were suppressed and their churches taken over by the Orthodox. Protestants formed a tiny minority, some of whom held out for true Christianity.

Laszlo Tokes was one of these. This pastor of the Hungarian Reformed Church took a tiny, lifeless congregation and quickly gained immense popularity by restoring proper spirit, priorities, and functions in the church. Tokes believed that if the people stopped thinking of their faith as just a Sunday morning ritual, if they understood that the church was the community of God's people that could infiltrate the world with the gospel, the church could become the vital force among the people that it should be.

The communist authorities were aghast, and attempted to shut him down. The bishop, a puppet of the communists, officially suspended him from ministry, yet Tokes kept preaching the truth and exposing the lies or the communist government—and his stubborn congregation continued to grow. So, after barbaric tactics to force him out of the pastorate failed, the communists ordered him to be exiled to a small, remote village outside of Timisoara. Tokes said to his congregation, all of whom faced dreadful persecution merely for attending his church, "Dear brothers and sisters in Christ, I have been issued a summons of eviction. I will not accept it, so I will be taken from you by force next Friday. They want to do this in secret because they have no right to do it. Please, come next Friday and be witnesses of what will happen. Come, be peaceful, but be witnesses."

Word spread throughout the city, and on the day of his eviction, Tokes looked out and saw a large crowd. "These were not only my parishioners, with a few Baptists and Adventists, but Orthodox priests and some of their Romanian flocks. I was very moved, and it changed what I now saw as my old prejudices—that we cannot make common cause, cannot fight side by side. Now that I have seen Romanians, Germans, Catholics, and Orthodox defending me, I know that I have to work for reconciliation between the nationalities and creeds in this country." He called out in Hungarian and then in Romanian: "We are one in Christ. We speak different languages, but we have the same Bible and the same God. We are one."

As night fell the authorities had not dared to remove Tokes because of the crowd. After one o'clock in the morning, someone had gotten hundreds of candles that people lighted in peaceful vigilance. This extraordinary demonstration continued throughout the night and into the following day. For the first time in their lives, Romanians shouted their secret dreams. "Liberty! Freedom!" Students began singing a forbidden patriotic song, "Awake, Romania!" Others shouted, "Down with Ceausescu! Down with communism!"

At dawn on December 17, the secret police broke into Tokes's home and beat him until his face was bloody. Then they took him and his wife, Edith, away into the night. A huge crowd moved to the central square of Timisoara, shouting and singing. As night fell, the candles came out again. The communists responded with the brutal force latent within that worldview, and opened fire into the crowd. Hundreds of people were shot.

This set in motion a shock wave that thundered throughout the nation of Romania, and before it was over, Romania was free and Ceausescu was gone. Churches filled with worshipers praising God. One of the pastors visited the hospital ward where one of the Christians was taken after he was shot. The boy was still recuperating, his wounds bandaged, and a stump where his left leg had been shot off, but his spirit was not shattered.

"Pastor," he said, "I don't mind so much the loss of my leg. After all, it was I who lit the first candle" (Summarized from *The Body*, 51–61).

Ceausescu could not stamp out the church. In the early part of the Roman Empire the Caesars tried to extinguish Christianity. They could not. In the middle nineteenth century, as godless totalitarianism swept across the world, godless leaders tried to stamp out Christianity. They could not. In Ethiopia, perhaps the oldest Christianized nation in the world, ruthless dictators tried to crush the church. But the dictators were finally deposed and the church is alive, stronger than ever before.

In the Soviet Union, Stalin tried to stamp out Christianity. For seventy years, the boot of oppression was laid to the neck of the church. For seventy years the communists closed church doors, turning them into museums and town halls, thinking they could get the people to forget about church. They could not. For seventy years, they taught the schoolchildren that there was no God, thinking that if they got to the children young enough and told them often enough that there was no God, they could stamp out the memory of God. They could not.

Seventy years later, the iron curtain fell, the Berlin wall came down, and the communist leaders are a dark shadow in history. The boot was taken off the neck of the church and there has been a turning to Christ on a scale never witnessed before in Russia.

Mao tried to stamp out Christianity as part of his revolution in China. He could not. Though Christianity in China is still under communist oppression, modern communication technology has enabled us to learn that there are multiplied millions of Christians in China. Oppressors and revilers of the church come and go, but the church remains. It is an anvil that has broken many hammers. Therefore, throughout history, we have seen the Holy Spirit supply the power and strength to the church in difficult situations so that the church thrives, rather than withers, under adversity.

Do you still think the church is weak, misdirected, and irrelevant? No, the church is not. Our misguided folly in watering the church down to our own abilities and our own expectations can cause the church to appear weak and misguided. But when we see the church for what it really is, we ought to lower our heads in humility. We don't deserve to walk beside those people who have looked sacrifice, deprivation, and even death in the face and have not flinched. And as a result, the earth trembled. These are people of whom the Bible says, "the world was not worthy" (Hebrews 11:38). When we see weakness and misdirection in the church, it is only because we are looking at ourselves in the mirror. If we allow Jesus to function as the head of the church, we see a powerful, dynamic, and visionary entity against which the gates of hell will never prevail.

SPEED BUMP!

Slow down to be sure you have gotten the main points of this chapter.

Q1. What is the universal church?

A1. The universal church is made up of all true *Christians* everywhere, past, present, and future.

Q2. How is the universal church pictured in Scripture?

A2. The universal church is pictured in Scripture by a *body,* a building, and a bride.

Q3. What is the local church?

A3. A local church is a group of believers who agree together to pursue the *ideals* of the universal church.

FILL IN THE BLANK

Q1. What is the universal church?

A1. The universal church is made up of all true _____ everywhere, past, present, and future.

Q2. How is the universal church pictured in Scripture?

A2. The universal church is pictured in Scripture by a _____ , a building, and a bride.

Q3. What is the local church?

A3. A local church is a group of believers who agree together to pursue the
_____of the universal church.

FOR FURTHER THOUGHT AND DISCUSSION

1. Before you read this chapter, if someone had asked you what a church was, what would you have answered?

2. If you could wave a magic wand and have a local church be exactly how you would like it to be, what would it be like?

3. How well do you do at fulfilling the "one anothers"? How well does your church do? Why do you think the church is not more "one another" oriented? What do you think we could do to improve our commitment to one another?

4. How healthy would your local church be if everyone had the same appreciation for, and level of commitment to it that you have?

WHAT IF I DON'T BELIEVE?

1. If I don't believe that membership in Christ's true church is gained by being a true Christian, I might be deceived into thinking that I can be a Christian simply by being a member of a local church somewhere.

2. If I don't believe that the church is a divine institution against which the "gates of hell will not prevail," I might not realize that Christ's true church is succeeding, in spite of the failures of some local churches.

3. If I don't believe that the church is a "covenant community," I am not likely to make the level of commitment to the church that Scripture expects of me. Nor am I as likely to turn to the church for help in my own times of need.

4. If I do not understand how important the church is to God, it will not be important enough to me.

FOR FURTHER STUDY

1. Scripture

- Matthew 16:13–18
- Acts 14:21–23
- Romans 12:4–5
- Ephesians 1:21–23
- Ephesians 2:19–22
- Ephesians 4:11–16
- Hebrews 10:24–25
- 1 Peter 2:4–8
- 1 Peter 4:10

2. Books

Several other books are very helpful for studying this subject further. They are listed below in general order of difficulty. If I could read only one of these, I would read the first one.

Know What You Believe, Paul Little

The Body, Charles Colson

The Bride, Charles Swindoll

The Walk, Gene Getz

The Church at the End of the Twentieth Century, Francis Schaeffer

2
WHAT DOES THE CHURCH BELIEVE?

It's about time for Christians who recite the creed and mean it to come together for fellowship and witness regardless of denominational identity.

—J. I. Packer

Max, why are there so many different denominations?" Bobby* shouted across the barbershop. "I mean, if there is only one God and only one Bible, why are there so many different churches? The Baptists believe one thing, the Methodists believe another thing, and the Presbyterians believe something else. I can't figure it out!"

Bobby was a good old boy who cut hair in the town where I used to live. He was interested in discussing spiritual things, and often did so at the top of his lungs, in the presence of current and waiting customers. He viewed me as quite a valuable resource to question about Christianity in the safe environment of his barber shop.

Whenever I walked into his shop, Bobby often greeted me with some question about Christianity. I loved it. Sometimes he would say something like, "Max, how do you get to heaven? If you have to be good to get to heaven, how good do you have to be? Do I have to give up drinking? Do I have to quit cussing? Do I have to give a bunch of money to that sorry church down the street? What do I have to do to get to heaven?"

Then, I would explain to Bobby, in the hearing of everyone in the shop, the way of salvation by grace through faith in Jesus.

But the one question Bobby always returned to in the years I got my hair cut there was why there were so many different denominations. I don't know if he would forget that I had already answered that question the year before, or whether he just wanted to hear it again. In the seven or eight years I got my hair cut there, I probably answered that question to the whole barbershop audience half a dozen times. If there is only one God and only one Bible, why are there so many different denominations?

(*Not his real name.)

WHAT YOU NEED TO KNOW ABOUT THE CHURCH

IN THIS CHAPTER WE LEARN THAT . . .

1. The Apostles' Creed is an ancient statement of the essentials of the Christian faith.

2. God the Father is the sovereign Creator of the universe.

3. Jesus of Nazareth is the Son of God and Savior of humanity.

4. The Holy Spirit is God, the third member of the Trinity, and helper of all Christians.

5. The universal church is the totality of all believers in Jesus from all places and all times.

6. Personal salvation is the experience by which a person by grace through faith in Jesus is forgiven of sins and given eternal life.

What Bobby was really asking was, "Why don't Christians all believe the same thing?" His question seems logical. There *is* only one God, and there *is* only one Bible. However, the Bible is a big book, and many complex issues in it are not presented so specifically that it eliminates the possibility of different responsible interpretations.

For example, the Bible makes it pretty clear that followers of Jesus should be baptized, but it does not make it *as* clear *how* they are to be baptized. For the answer to that, you have to study the individual words very carefully, take into account historical and cultural use, as well as customs in literature outside the Bible, and then make some educated guesses. So, some churches sprinkle water on the head. Some pour water on the head with water cupped in the minister's hand, or poured from a small container. Others, however, really get into it and immerse the entire person in water. Why? Because they believe that that is what it means to "baptize."

But even among those who immerse, there is little agreement. Some immerse the person one time backward, while others immerse the person three times forward (once in the name of the Father, once in the name of the Son, and once in the name of the Holy Spirit). If you only ever heard one person explain baptism, you would think it was clear from the Bible. However, all you have to do is hear someone else, and things are not so clear. I think I have heard or read every explanation there is for how to baptize, and every one seemed plausible to me at the moment I heard or read it.

Similar lack of agreement exists on the subjects of church government, eternal security, the free will of man versus the sovereignty of God, and so on.

However, for all the things Christians do not agree on, there are several on which they do agree. We want to focus, in this chapter, on the things we all agree on, and to do that, we will use the Apostles' Creed as our model. When we talk about the Apostles' Creed, that is one thing we can say the church believes.

WHAT IS THE APOSTLES' CREED?

The Apostles' Creed is an ancient statement of the essentials of the Christian faith.

For hundreds of years, Christians believed that the twelve apostles wrote the Apostles' Creed, and that is, of course, where the statement of faith got its name. Most scholars today, however, agree that that is not the case. However, they agree that it is certainly consistent with what the apostles believed and taught, and that they would be in full agreement with it. Creed means "belief," and this creed certainly articulates what the apostles believed.

A briefer form of the Apostles' Creed, called the Roman Creed, dates back nearly to the time of the apostles. A few statements were added to the Roman Creed to make sure people did not drift off into false teaching. The statement as it exists now is about thirteen hundred years old. When you quote the Apostles' Creed today, you are quoting something that was almost certainly quoted by Martin Luther, John Calvin, John and Charles Wesley, and many other great figures in church history.

THE APOSTLES' CREED

I believe in God the Father Almighty,
maker of heaven and earth:
And in Jesus Christ His only Son, our Lord;
who was conceived by the Holy Spirit
born of the Virgin Mary,
suffered under Pontius Pilate,
was crucified, dead, and buried;
He descended into Hades;
the third day He rose again from the dead;
He ascended into heaven, and sitteth at the right hand of God,
the Father Almighty;
from there He shall come to judge the living and the dead.
I believe in the Holy Spirit,
the holy Christian church,
the communion of saints,
the forgiveness of sins,
the resurrection of the body,
and the life everlasting. Amen.

The creed has been used throughout the centuries for several purposes:

- A statement of faith prior to baptism
- A teaching outline
- A guard against heresy
- A part of personal and church worship
- A statement of faith for membership in a local church

The creed affirms everything that historically has been considered essential in order to be truly Christian. The earnest Christian will believe more than is in the Apostles' Creed, since it is not an exhaustive statement of faith, but he will not believe less.

It has been a comfort throughout the ages for Christians to be able to consult a brief statement of what it means to be a Christian, and to know that the same statement has been affirmed by the giants of the faith for centuries.

The Apostles' Creed makes a fundamental statement of Christian belief regarding five subjects, which will form the outline for the remainder of the chapter:

1. God the Father
2. God the Son
3. God the Holy Spirit
4. The church
5. Personal salvation

WHO IS GOD THE FATHER?

God the Father is the sovereign Creator of the universe.

I believe in . . . . Many people who live like the devil say they believe in God. It is particularly common today, when we are so good at separating what we say we believe from how we live, for many high-profile people (movie stars, television stars, professional athletes, and politicians) to say they believe in God. I heard one female rock star who said she believed in God, yet she has done more to trash the morals of a teenage generation than almost any other female performer in history. She does not "believe in" God in the biblical sense. She may believe God exists, and may even have benevolent feelings toward Him, but when the Bible talks about "believing," it means not only believing that God exists, but also making a life commitment to Him, to obey Him, and to commit oneself to becoming like Him.

In the original language of the New Testament, the Greek word for "believe" is the Greek word *pisteuo*, which carries with it the idea of *commitment*. John 2:24 says that a crowd of people who heard Jesus were responding to His teaching, "But Jesus did not commit Himself to them, because He knew all men." Without getting bogged down in a discussion of what the passage means, we simply want to make the observation that the word "commit" is the same word as "believe." The two concepts are so much a part of the word *pisteuo* that it can be translated either "believe" or "commit."

When, in the spirit of the Apostles' Creed, we say we believe in God, we are saying that we are entrusting ourselves to Him. It means more than to believe that God exists. It means more than to believe certain truths *about* God. Rather, it means that I am living in a relationship of *commitment* to God. When I say, "I believe in God," I am declaring my belief that the God of the Bible has invited me to a relationship with Him that involves commitment to Him, and I am declaring that I have accepted His invitation. If a person does not mean all that, then he has no basis for standing up in public and declaring that he believes in God. He does not believe what the Apostles' Creed is saying. The same is true, of course, when we say we believe in Jesus Christ and the Holy Spirit.

> **The earnest Christian will believe more than is in the Apostles' Creed, but certainly not less.**

God the Father, Almighty. When we say we believe in God, we do not believe in just any higher power. One of the steps of the Alcoholics Anonymous' Twelve-Step Program is to acknowledge your dependence on a higher power. In order to make the Twelve-Step Program as acceptable to as many people as possible, they do not define who this higher power is. Therefore, Christians, Jews, Muslims, New Agers, Satan worshipers, and anyone else that they need who believes in a higher power can participate in Alcoholics Anonymous.

The God of the Bible is not just a higher power, however. He defines Himself, gives Himself a name, and describes His character and actions. He is an exclusive God. If you worship Him, you can worship no other. As God, He is all-knowing, all-powerful, and present everywhere simultaneously. He is holy, loving, just, good, and merciful. He is the God of Israel, and He sent His Son, Jesus, to die for the sins of the world.

His name is Jehovah (or YHWH), as He told Moses when Moses met Him at the burning bush. The name means "I am who I am," or "I will be what I will be" (Exodus 3:13ff RSV; see text and margin note). His name means that He cannot be hindered from being what He is and doing what He wills.

WHY I NEED TO KNOW THIS

Unless I understand how profoundly significant it is to affirm the Apostles' Creed, I will probably recite it without as much meaning as I should when I say it. Affirming the Apostles' Creed has widespread ramifications in a person's life, and unless I grasp that, I will glibly mouth it in future worship services without letting it impact my life the way it should.

We can also make the broader observation that the creed declares belief in the Trinity, which means "one God eternally existing in three co-equal and co-eternal persons." God the Father, God the Son, and God the Holy Spirit are the three persons who make up the one God. This is a difficult truth, and one that we cannot fully explore in this chapter, but one that deserves to be stated for the record. (For a fuller discussion of the Trinity, see the book *What You Need to Know about God*.)

A final observation we can make about the Almighty is that, while God can do anything He chooses, He will never choose to do anything contrary to His character or His will. For example, God cannot make a round square. That is an inherent contradiction and violates the character of God, since He is not a God of inherent contradictions or nonsense. Nor will God overrule His will. He has decreed that certain things shall occur, and will not overrule that decree. He is able to do whatever He wills, but has already determined what that should be.

Maker of heaven and earth. This statement affirms that the earth is not the result of a big bang in an eternal lump of matter at the center of the universe. We are not a product of "nothing + the impersonal + time + chance." The theory of evolution does not explain the existence of "what is." There is a Maker of heaven and earth, a Creator who is responsible for the existence of the universe and the presence of humanity. The modern Western world has a puny concept of God, but that doesn't change anything about God. No matter what we say about God, it makes no difference unless God says the same thing. To state that we believe in God the Father Almighty, maker *of heaven and earth*, we are affirming that He is greater than we, beyond our ability to grasp, and deserving of our respect and worship. It puts God in His proper place in our minds.

It also puts the earth in its proper place. Certainly, humanity has fouled the planet in a most ungodly way, and we had better begin to clean it up not only to honor our Creator, but also if we don't want more trouble than the world has ever seen before. However, the earth is not our mother. We are not "one" with the earth. God is not the earth and the earth is not God. Many of the New Age and pantheistic notions about the earth that are being promoted are patently unbiblical. God created the earth. He is distinct from it. God created humanity, which is distinct from the earth. The earth is under the stewardship of humanity, which, admittedly, has abused it terribly. But to make humanity the servant of the earth is not a correct solution to the environmental problem. All this swings into perspective when we affirm the Apostles' Creed.

WHO IS JESUS?

Jesus of Nazareth is the Son of God and Savior of humanity.

I believe in . . . Jesus Christ His only Son, our Lord. This affirmation is a bone that sticks in the craw of many people. When the Apostles' Creed declares that God the Father is "maker of heaven and earth," it parts company with all Eastern religions, such as Hinduism, Buddhism, Confucianism, and pantheism. Now, by calling Jesus God's *only Son*, it parts company with the other two great religions of the world, Judaism and Islam. The Bible's insistence that Jesus is the Son of God and the only way of salvation makes Christianity a very exclusive religion, a fact that bothers many people exceedingly. The Bible teaches this exclusivity very clearly, however, and the Apostles' Creed affirms it.

Jesus is the Greek name for Joshua, meaning "God is savior." It is His "given name" whereby He became known as the son of Joseph and Mary, a carpenter who grew up in Nazareth of Galilee. Then, He was a traveling preacher for three years before He was put to death by Pontius Pilate in about A.D. 30.

Christ refers to Jesus' role as the Messiah, the "sent one of God" who came in fulfillment of Old Testament prophecy to die so that He could offer salvation to those who believed in Him and received Him by faith.

> The Bible insists that Jesus is the Son of God and the only way of salvation.

The phrase *our Lord* affirms that Jesus is God who became a human being and lived among us (John 1:14), and because of His divine nature, has the authority and right to rule over us, and to receive our worship and obedience. When we affirm all this about Jesus, the intent of the creed is that we are announcing our commitment to Jesus, just as we earlier announced our commitment to God the Father Almighty. Unless we have believed in Jesus in the same sense as we believed in God earlier, and have committed our lives to Him, we have no basis for saying publicly that we believe in Jesus Christ. We do not just agree that a person named Jesus of Nazareth lived. We agree that He is God, that He has a right to rule over our lives, and that we must willingly submit to His authority over us.

He was **conceived by the Holy Spirit,** which allowed Him to be human without being contaminated by the sin that contaminates the rest of humanity. This balance of truths is critical, because if Jesus were not human, He could not have died, and if He were not God, it would not have mattered if He had died. His death would not be sufficient to forgive our sins. Because Jesus lived a sinless human life and died innocently, His death could be substituted for another person. Because He was God, who is infinite, His death could count for all humanity. Therefore, when we believe in and receive Jesus as our Savior, His death is substituted for ours, we escape spiritual death, and we are free to go to heaven when we die.

> Jesus' victory over death assures our forgiveness, our resurrection, and eternal fellowship with God and all other believers.

Born of the Virgin Mary. There are two common misconceptions about Jesus. One is that He was God without being fully human. And the other is that He was human without being fully God. When we affirm that He is *Jesus Christ our Lord*, we testify that He was God. When we affirm that He was *born of the Virgin Mary*, we testify that He was human. This statement was probably added by ancient church fathers to offset the heresy that Jesus was God without being human. Some people taught that He was an angel or a ghost. This affirmation puts that error to rest. Jesus was both God and human.

When we affirm that Jesus was *conceived by the Holy Spirit and born of the Virgin Mary*, we testify to our belief in both the full deity and full humanity of Jesus, and avoid the heresies about Jesus that have come and gone throughout the centuries.

Suffered under Pontius Pilate, was crucified, dead, and buried. To say that Jesus was crucified is the cultural equivalent today of saying that someone was executed in the electric chair. Today, it is common for people to wear jewelry in the shape of crosses, and to adorn homes, cars, and offices with crosses. Yet to those living in the Roman Empire, this would seem as out of place as wearing a gold electric chair around our necks would seem today. Crucifixion was merely a cruel means of execution for those who were not Roman citizens. Condemned Roman citizens were given the considerably more humane treatment of being beheaded.

Jesus, then, was crucified under the authority of Pontius Pilate, who was the Roman governor over the city of Jerusalem at the time. As He hung on the cross, soldiers came by to break Jesus' legs, to hasten death by asphyxiation, but when they came to Him, He appeared to be dead. A soldier stuck a spear into His side, and out came blood and water, a sure medical sign that He was already dead, and so they did not break His legs (thus fulfilling an Old Testament prophecy in Psalm 34:20).

He was then buried in a tomb before nightfall. We affirm the clear testimony of Scripture in this part of the creed, and eliminate any nonsense that would water down the reality of His crucifixion and death.

He descended into Hades. Hades was the place of the departed dead, not the final resting place of the godless, commonly known today as hell. Some versions of the Apostles' Creed say that Jesus descended into hell, but that is a consequence of the word *hell* having changed its meaning since the English form of the creed was established. That Jesus descended into Hades means that He died, and it was from a genuine death that He arose.

This clause, *He descended into Hades*, was not made part of the Apostles' Creed until the fourth century after Jesus' birth, and as a result, it is not used by some churches whose liturgy was established on an older form of the creed.

Because Jesus really died, and overcame that death, we can have the confidence that when we who trust in Christ die, we too shall overcome death.

The third day He rose again from the dead. That Jesus rose again from the dead is extremely important for three reasons:

1. He said He would rise again from the dead (Matthew 28:6). If He didn't, He would have been a fraud, and everything He taught and promised would be suspect.

2. If Christ has not been raised, your faith is worthless; you are still in your sins (1 Corinthians 15:17).

3. If He did not rise from the dead, there is no reason to hope that we will. We may go into an eternal sleep, or worse yet, fall into torment. Who knows what lies beyond the grave if Jesus did not rise from the dead!

On the other hand, if Jesus did rise from the dead, then

1. Jesus is the Son of God (Romans 1:4).

2. Jesus has victory over death (Acts 2:24).

3. Jesus' victory over death assures the Christian of his forgiveness and imputed righteousness (1 Corinthians 15:17; Romans 4:25).

4. Jesus guarantees the Christian's own resurrection (1 Corinthians 15:18).

(Evidence for the resurrection of Jesus is discussed in another book in this series, *What You Need to Know about Jesus*.)

James Packer wrote in his book *Growing in Christ,*

Suppose that Jesus, having died on the cross, had stayed dead. Suppose that, like Socrates or Confucius, he was now no more than a beautiful memory. Would it matter? We should still have his example and teaching; wouldn't they be enough? Enough for what? Not for Christianity. Had Jesus not risen, but stayed dead, the bottom would drop out of Christianity. (59)

It is certainly a wonderful thing to be able to affirm this marvelous truth, knowing that, if we have meant all previous affirmations in the creed, we can voice this one with joyful confidence.

He ascended into heaven. Forty days after Jesus' resurrection, He gathered with His disciples on the Mount of Olives just outside Jerusalem, not far from the Garden of Gethsemane, and after having a few words with them, "while they watched, He was taken up, and a cloud received Him out of their sight" (Acts 1:9).

The apostle Paul tells us that God

raised Him from the dead and seated Him at His right hand in the heavenly places, far above all principality and power and might and dominion, and every name that is named, not only in this age but also in that which is to come. And He put all things under His feet, and gave Him to be head over all things to the church, which is His body, the fullness of Him who fills all in all. (Ephesians 1:20–23)

Jesus, then, is in heaven at the right hand of God, possessing full power and authority to execute God's will and fulfill His promises. That He is "seated" means His work is completed. That He is "at the right hand of God" means He has a position of power and authority. It is symbolic of the fact that His atoning work as High Priest is finished once for all.

From there He shall come to judge the living (quick) and the dead. From Jesus' position of power and authority, He will return one day. With His coming, Scripture tells us, will come our bodily resurrection and the full measure of eternal life that is promised to us (Matthew 25:31–46; John 5:25–29; Romans 8:18–24; Revelation 20:11—21:4).

This is the great hope for all Christians, the final day when all will be set right, a day all Christians may anticipate with great eagerness. On the other hand, it is a terrifying specter for those who are not Christians.

Jesus warned us to "be ready, for the Son of Man is coming at an hour you do not expect" (Matthew 24:44). For the non-Christian, this means to accept everything in the creed up to this, and commit oneself to it. For the Christian, it means to keep short accounts with God, to live with Him in an attitude of faithful obedience.

Someone has said, "Plan as though Jesus were not coming in your lifetime, but live as though He were coming tomorrow." When Jesus comes, He should find us praying for revival and planning for participating in world evangelism, but packed up, as it were, and ready to leave at the same time.

WHO IS THE HOLY SPIRIT?

The Holy Spirit is God, the third member of the Trinity, and helper of all Christians.

I believe in the Holy Spirit. The Holy Spirit acts like God throughout the Bible, is mentioned in the same breath as the Father and Son, and is indirectly called God. If all Scriptures are taken at face value, a picture emerges of a living person, divine and co-equal with the Father and the Son, distinct but not separate from them. His work in the New Testament is to glorify Jesus. Of the Holy Spirit in the Scriptures, we read that

- He was involved in original creation (Genesis 1:2).
- He inspired God's spokesmen and ensured that the Bible was the Word of God (Isaiah 61:6; 2 Timothy 3:16–17; 2 Peter 1:20).
- He conceived Jesus (Matthew 1:20).
- He filled Jesus (Luke 4:1, 14, 18).
- He is the helper for Christians (John 16:7).
- He causes the fruit of the Spirit to grow in us (Galatians 5:22–23).
- He does not glorify Himself, but will take what is Jesus' and declare it to us (John 16:14).
- He gives each Christian a spiritual gift for mutual ministry to others (Ephesians 4:11–16).
- He is called, indirectly, God (Acts 5:1–4).
- He is mentioned in the same breath as the Father and Son (2 Corinthians 12:13).

By any reasonable measure, we must accept the Holy Spirit as God, the third member of the Trinity. If we accept Him as God, we must also accept the work He does, which includes convicting us of sin, enabling us to understand Scripture, leading us in righteousness, and gifting us to minister to others. (For a more complete discussion of the Holy Spirit, see the book in this series *What You Need to Know about the Holy Spirit*.)

WHAT IS THE UNIVERSAL CHURCH?

The universal church is the totality of all believers in Jesus from all places and all times.

I believe in . . . the holy Christian church. The original creed reads, "I believe in the holy catholic church." By this it does not single out the Roman Catholic Church, but rather refers to the worldwide fellowship of all believing people whose head is Christ. *Catholic* means, technically, "universal," so the original is merely a reference to the universal church. To avoid confusion, modernized versions have made the helpful revision of saying, "I believe in the holy Christian church." This is an affirmation of the belief in the universal church, the body and bride of Christ (Ephesians 2:19–22).

I believe in . . . the communion of saints. This phrase is an affirmation of the fact that all believers are part of the body of Christ, by virtue of that fact, have spiritual unity with all other Christians, and are called upon to manifest that unity in functional ways (Ephesians 4:3). It affirms the union in Christ of all members of the "church militant" on earth and the "church triumphant" in heaven. It may also mean that we have communion in things such as baptism, the Lord's Supper, the preaching of the Word, the worship of God, or corporate prayer.

WHAT IS PERSONAL SALVATION?

Personal salvation is the experience by which a person by grace through faith in Jesus is forgiven of sins and given eternal life.

I believe in . . . the forgiveness of sins. The Bible says that "all have sinned and fall short of the glory of God" (Romans 3:23) and that the "wages of sin is death" (Romans 6:23). That means that all have died, or been spiritually severed from God. Left to ourselves, we would be without hope, destined to eternal destruction (2 Thessalonians 1:9). But God, in His mercy, because of the great love with which He loved us, has provided a way for us to be forgiven of our sins, given new life, and restored to fellowship with God Himself. Theologian James Packer talks about the "glorious but" in Psalm 130:3–4, "If You, LORD, should mark iniquities, O Lord, who could stand? But there is forgiveness with You, that You may be feared [worshiped with reverence]." This is the great news of the gospel. Our sins can be forgiven. It is a profound privilege to be able to affirm this in the Apostles' Creed.

I believe in . . . the resurrection of the body. The one great problem in life is death. Death is the final insult, the great enemy. There is no problem greater than the problem of how to prepare for death. If death is final, then the only thing that makes sense on earth is to eat, drink, and be merry. If death is not final, and the possibility of judgment exists, then the only thing that makes sense is to try to discover how to escape that judgment.

The creed articulates the biblical teaching that frees us from death's dread. We can be resurrected, given new and eternal life in Christ. The fact that Jesus rose from the dead is the great hope we have that His children will, in fact, rise from the dead also, as He promised. The apostle Paul wrote that Jesus will "transform the body of our humble state into conformity with the body of His glory" (Philippians 3:21 NASB). In that day, "He will wipe away every tear from [our] eyes; and there will no longer be any death; there will no longer be any mourning, or crying, or pain" (Revelation 21:4 NASB). What a joy to those who have physical deformities or limitations or pain. What a joy to those who have grown old, watching their bodies deteriorate from strong, able specimens to weak, disease-riddled shells. One day this will all be left behind, and we will soar into heaven in a body like Jesus'.

> With life everlasting, the fairy tale comes true: Silly saved sinners live happily ever after, by God's mercy.

I believe in . . . the life everlasting. When the Apostles' Creed culminates with the affirmation of "life everlasting," it means not just endless existence, because Satan and his demons have that. Rather, it means the final, endless joy into which we enter in fellowship with the triune God. Jesus said, "Where I am, there My servant will be also" (John 12:26). Again, He prayed in John 17:24, "Father, I desire that they also whom You gave Me may be with Me where I am, that they may behold My glory."

Fellowship with God, being with Jesus, that is heaven. We will not sit on clouds and strum harps endlessly, trying to think of new tunes after a million years. Rather, we will worship, work, eat, think, create, fellowship, and enjoy the as yet unimaginable joys and pleasures of a place where God is, where there is no sin, and with no limitations on us as glorious creatures created in His image.

Think of the greatest moment in your life, or the greatest moment you could ever wish for yourself. Whatever it is, it comes to an end here on earth. In heaven, however, that moment will not only be surpassed, but that which surpasses it will never end.

CONCLUSION

Many years ago, in a *Peanuts* cartoon, Lucy and Linus were sitting in front of the TV set when Lucy said to Linus, "Go get me a glass of water."

Linus was taken aback and asked, "Why should I do anything for you?"

Lucy replied, "On your 75th birthday, I'll bake you a cake."

Linus got up, headed for the kitchen, and said, "Life is more pleasant when you have something to look forward to."

And so it is.

And heaven is a pretty wonderful place to look forward to. When we affirm the Apostle's Creed, we affirm in a deeply personal way not only our hope of heaven, but also every major truth on which true Christians have been agreed for two thousand years.

SPEED BUMP!

Slow down to be sure you have gotten the main points of this chapter.

Q1. What is the Apostles' Creed?

A1. The Apostles' Creed is an ancient statement of the *essentials* of the Christian faith.

Q2. Who is God the Father?

A2. God the Father is the sovereign *Creator* of the universe.

Q3. Who is Jesus?

A3. Jesus of Nazareth is the Son of God and *Savior* of humanity.

Q4. Who is the Holy Spirit?

A4. The Holy Spirit is God, the third member of the Trinity, and *helper* of all Christians.

Q5. What is the universal church?

A5. The universal church is the totality of all *believers* in Jesus from all places and all times.

Q6. What is personal salvation?

A6. Personal salvation is the experience by which a person by grace through faith in Jesus *is forgiven* of sins and given eternal life.

FILL IN THE BLANK

Q1. What is the Apostles' Creed?

A1. The Apostles' Creed is an ancient statement of the _____ of the Christian faith.

Q2. Who is God the Father?

A2. God the Father is the sovereign _____ of the universe.

Q3. Who is Jesus?

A3. Jesus of Nazareth is the Son of God and _____ of humanity.

Q4. Who is the Holy Spirit?

A4. The Holy Spirit is God, the third member of the Trinity, and _____ of all Christians.

Q5. What is the universal church?

A5. The universal church is the totality of all _____ in Jesus from all places and all times.

Q6. What is personal salvation?

A6. Personal salvation is the experience by which a person by grace through faith in Jesus is _____ of sins and given eternal life.

FOR FURTHER THOUGHT AND DISCUSSION

1. Had you heard the Apostles' Creed before reading this chapter? If not, how has it helped your understanding of the basics of Christianity? If so, how has your appreciation of the document been influenced?

2. How has your understanding changed of what it means to believe in God? When people say they believe in God, how many of them do you think mean it on the level that the Apostles' Creed means it? Is that how fully you mean it?

3. Does it bother you that the Bible is so exclusive when it says that Jesus is the only way of salvation? Why or why not?

4. Why do you think the concept of final judgment is so disagreeable to many people?

5. If you were to discover that you had brothers and sisters whom you didn't know you had, how do you think it would affect you? How does it affect you to reflect on the fact that you belong to the same spiritual family with all other Christians from all times and all places?

WHAT IF I DON'T BELIEVE?

If I don't believe the affirmations made in the Apostles' Creed at least about God and Jesus, I cannot be a Christian, I have no hope of life after death, and nothing to give me meaning while on this earth. All Christians believe more than what is mentioned in the Apostles' Creed, but we ought not to believe less. There are parts of the Apostles' Creed that a person might not have learned about yet and still be a Christian. But if a person knows the teachings of the creed and rejects it entirely, that person cannot be a Christian. It reflects the essence of Christianity.

FOR FURTHER STUDY

1. Scripture

- Genesis 1
- John 1:1–14
- John 3:16
- 2 Corinthians 12:13
- Ephesians 2:19–21
- Philippians 3:21
- Revelation 20:11–21:4

2. Books

Several other books are very helpful in studying this subject further. They are listed below in general order of difficulty. If I could read only one of these, I would read the first one.

Growing in Christ, James Packer

I Believe: Understanding and Applying the Apostles' Creed, Alister McGrath

God: Knowing Our Creator, Max Anders

Jesus: Knowing Our Savior, Max Anders

The Holy Spirit: Knowing Our Comforter, Max Anders

3

WHAT SHOULD THE CHARACTER OF THE CHURCH BE?

The chief trouble with the church is that you and I are in it.
—Charles Heimsath

The Great Wall of China is one of the marvels of the world. It was built to identify the border of China as well as to keep out invading Mongolian hordes. It is so massive and long that it is one of the few objects on earth that can be seen from space. The wall runs fifteen hundred miles from the Mongolian plateau in the west to the Yellow Sea. The wall varies from twelve to forty feet in width and from twenty to fifty feet in height! Imagine a stone wall approximately twenty feet wide and forty feet high running from New York City nearly to Denver, Colorado, and you get some idea of the magnitude of this astonishing structure.

And was it effective in keeping out the invading hordes? Well, yes and no. It was effective in that no invasion ever climbed over, broke down, or went around the wall. However, the Manchu conquerors of the Ming dynasty simply bribed a gate-keeper who opened the gate wide and allowed them to walk through. The flaw in the Chinese defense was placing too much reliance on the wall and not giving enough attention to the character of the people guarding the wall.

So it is with our personal defenses. On the whole, most readers of this book would not be liars or cheaters or stealers. Most of us have an adequate wall of character built around our lives. But we all have weak spots, and those weak spots must be given as much as or more attention than our strong spots. What value is there if we would *never* embezzle funds from our employer, but our life is destroyed because we commit adultery? No, total character is important. It may be that our life is only as secure as our weakest character trait.

IN THIS CHAPTER WE LEARN THAT . . .

1. Faith is believing what God has said and acting accordingly.

2. Hope is putting your confidence in the future.

3. Love is the exercise of my will for the good of another.

Just as character is important for individuals, so it is also important for institutions. For a number of years, I traveled a great deal, speaking in a different church almost every weekend. I learned that each church had a personality, a corporate character. Sometimes the church was a happy church, quick to laugh. Other times it was a sober church, slow to laugh, but quick to see deeper truths. Still other times it was a critical church, quick to say something sarcastic or cutting.

Sometimes this "corporate character" was a reflection of a pastor who had been at the church for a very long time. Other times, it was a result of a core of laypeople who had made up the backbone of the church for many years. Still other times, the character was a reflection of denominational ties. But just as a person has a character, so a church has a character.

Francis Schaeffer once said that we ought to examine our values and behavior very carefully, because we catch our values and behavior the same way we catch the measles—by being around others who have them; and upon reflection, we might actually prefer different values and behavior. That statement had a profound effect on me. Nearly thirty years later, I can still vividly remember being struck with the realization that I could change—that I could be different, more than I was. That was the beginning of a time of significant change in my life brought on by the ministry of the Holy Spirit.

> Faith, hope, and love: three crucial characteristics each church must possess.

I believe a group of people can do the same. Specifically, I believe a church can change. But what would a church aspire to? If a church wanted to be different or more, what would it be?

The Scripture helps here, because I believe the Scripture gives not only individuals, but also churches, a picture of what their character ought to be. There are three words in Scripture that are repeated over and over again as characteristics a church does, or ought to, possess. These characteristics, as separate entities, are common to all of us, but learning how they relate to a local church was something I heard for the first time in seminary from Dr. Gene Getz, a professor of mine, who later recorded his insights on the matter in his book *The Walk*. These three character traits for a local church are faith, hope, and love.

We see in many of the letters to churches in the New Testament the observation that churches do possess these three characteristics or ought to. Perhaps the most powerful statement concerning these three characteristics is found in 1 Corinthians 13:13: "Now abide faith, hope, love, these three; but the greatest of these is love."

However, we also see them in letters to other churches.

> For this reason I too, having heard of the **faith** in the Lord Jesus which exists among you and your **love** for all the saints, do not cease giving thanks for you, while making mention of you in my prayers; . . . that you will know what is the **hope** of His calling. (Ephesians 1:15–16, 18 NASB)

> We give thanks to the God and Father of our Lord Jesus Christ, praying always for you, since we heard of your **faith** in Christ Jesus and of your **love** for all the saints; because of the **hope** which is laid up for you in heaven. (Colossians 1:3–5)

> We give thanks to God always for you all, making mention of you in our prayers, remembering without ceasing your work of **faith**, labor of **love**, and patience of **hope** in our Lord Jesus Christ in the sight of our God and Father. (1 Thessalonians 1:2–3)

Paul frequently mentioned two or three of these characteristics in the opening of his letters to churches. That is why it seems reasonable to conclude that these are three marks he wants to be true of the corporate character of a local church.

Seeing then that these three characteristics are defining characteristics for a healthy local church, we will look more closely at each one.

WHAT IS FAITH?

Faith is believing what God has said and acting accordingly.

If the Bible is true, then we must do something about it. James 2:17: "Faith by itself, if it does not have works, is dead." We must change our personal character, and we must try to change the world in which we live. The gospel is so amazing, so astonishing a truth that it cannot be kept to oneself, any more than a limitless source of water could be kept a secret from people dying of thirst.

Chuck Colson, in his book *Faith on the Line*, tells the story of how faith changed the way people looked at themselves and the world in which they lived.

In a prison in New Mexico, all six men on death row had become Christians. The youngest, only eighteen, told Colson, "I'm ready to die; I'm ready to be with

Jesus. But before I die I want to make a film on the problem of child sexual molestation, because I am a victim. I want to leave something that will be shown in schools to tell kids how to deal with it."

No longer preoccupied only with himself, this forgiven and changed murderer was trying to find one last act of "good" he could do before he went into eternity. That is faith in action.

During a Prison Fellowship seminar in Kentucky, eight prisoners walked forward and made professions of faith in Christ. Then, inmates filled a galvanized horse tank with water and baptized them in the presence of all the prisoners. Some jeered. Others watched intently. Because of Christ, those eight men had the courage to take a stand for Him in prison where doing so is not merely a witness; it is a risk to their lives. That is faith in action.

Some years ago, Jack Eckerd, founder of Eckerd Drugs, came to Christ. The first thing he did was to take *Playboy* and *Penthouse* magazines out of the stores. Managers protested, "We're making a huge profit selling those magazines."

Eckerd replied, "I don't care. Take those magazines out of my stores." That is faith in action.

In Belfast, Northern Ireland, torn by sectarian strife between Catholics and Protestants, Liam, a Catholic, nearly died on a hunger strike. When his mother persuaded him to break it, he realized he had to make a choice between his cause—the Irish Republican Army—and Jesus. He chose Jesus, and his faith led him to radical steps of forgiveness and love.

He reached out to his former enemies, and Jimmy, a former Protestant terrorist, came to know Christ. At a Prison Fellowship seminar, Liam said, "Before, if I had seen Jimmy on the street, I would have shot him. Now he's my brother in Christ. I would die for him!" That is faith in action (66–69).

If we believe the Bible, it demands that we do something. If it says we should change, we must change. If it says we must go into all the world and preach the gospel, we must go. If it says we should preach the word faithfully, we must preach it. If

WHY I NEED TO KNOW THIS

It has been said that if you don't know what you are aiming for, you have very little chance of hitting it. So it is with the church. If we don't know what God expects of a church, in terms of its character, we are not likely to be very effective in manifesting it. Also, since a church is made up of people, we, ourselves, must manifest the same character traits as the church as a whole should. Otherwise we may be part of the problem in the church, rather than part of the solution.

it says we must worship God in spirit and in truth, then we must worship. Faith is a matter of finding out what God says and doing it.

Faith also means we cannot give up what we believe, if indeed we believe it. Persecution, ridicule, discrimination may come, but a living, dynamic faith remains true—not without struggle, perhaps, but in the end, it remains true.

Perhaps we may not be faced with such towering experiences as Chuck Colson in a prison, or Jack Eckerd in a national, multimillion-dollar business. But the principles are the same for us all. We may not risk our lives to share our faith with others, or to let others know that we are Christians. But we may risk our reputation as a businessperson or salesman or PTA member. We may risk embarrassment to share Christ with a neighbor. We may risk our comfort zone to minister to the needy on Thanksgiving rather than watch parades and football on television.

> **True faith urges us to personal risk for Christ's sake.**

Or, like Jack Eckerd, we may need to make some decisions that cost us money because of our faith. Perhaps we will decide to shop at a more expensive grocery store because they do not carry pornographic magazines. Or maybe we will buy our gas from a service station operated by a faithful believer, even though we could buy it for a couple cents cheaper per gallon down the street, where the cheaper gas is subsidized by profits from smut.

Not all decisions of faith are monumental. Many Christians never let others outside their church know that they are Christians, and many never do anything to encourage Christian principles in the world if it costs them any money. We must try to determine what the Bible says and do it, whether it is a big thing like putting our life on the line by declaring publicly in prison that we are a Christian, or whether it is a small thing like putting our ego on the line by declaring publicly at a PTA meeting that we are a Christian.

WHAT IS HOPE?

Hope is putting your confidence in the future.

Christians are faced with decisions on whether or not to remain faithful, and when they do, their hope often makes the difference. There is a clear link between faith and hope. What causes Christians to suffer for Christ's sake? It is hope, eternal hope in Jesus Christ. They realize that this earth is not their home; they are just passing through. They are strangers here, sojourners. Their real home is in heaven.

Out of this hope, the apostle Paul wrote from prison, "For to me, to live is Christ, and to die is gain" (Philippians 1:21). He knew that if the broad-bladed ax of the Roman government fell to the back of his neck, he would have a home in heaven. "For we know that if our earthly house, this tent, is destroyed, we have a building from God, a house not made with hands, eternal in the heavens" (2 Corinthians 5:1).

In Corrie ten Boom's book *Tramp for the Lord*, she has a chapter entitled "A Strange Place to Hope." In this chapter she tells the story of being taken to Ravensbruk, a dreadful concentration camp in Germany during World War II. She and her sister, Betsie, had been arrested for aiding and abetting Jews in their home in Holland. The first thing the authorities did was take away all personal belongings, and dress everyone in prison clothing. This was a terrifying prospect, since they desperately wanted to preserve their most cherished possession, a small Bible. She tied the Bible to a string around her neck to try to hide it. Then, Corrie wrote,

> Of course when I put on the flimsy prison dress, the Bible bulged beneath it. But that was [God's] business, not mine. At the exit, guards were [searching] every prisoner, front, back and sides. I prayed, "Oh, Lord, send your angels to surround us." But then I remembered that angels are spirits and you can see through them. What I needed was an angel to shield me so the guards could not see me. "Lord," I prayed again, "make your angels un-transparent." How unorthodox you can pray when you are in great need! But God did not mind. He did it.
>
> The woman ahead of me was searched. Behind me, Betsie was searched. They did not touch or even look at me. It was as though I was blocked out of their sight.
>
> So Betsie and I came to our barracks at Ravensbruk. Before long we were holding clandestine Bible study groups for an evergrowing group of believers, and Barracks 28 became known throughout the camp as "the crazy place, where they hope."
>
> Yes, hoped, in spite of all that human madness could do. We had learned that a stronger power had the final word, even here. (16–17)

Alexander Pope has written, "Hope springs eternal in the human breast." And so it does. We live on hope. We prosper on hope. We survive on hope. When we lose hope, we die. Those who commit suicide do so because they lose hope that their present pain, which they feel is intolerable, will ever be relieved. As long as you have hope you can hang on. Without it, you let go.

Corrie and her fellow Christians hoped. They placed their hope in the fact that God would see them through the torment of their circumstances, and that when they died (as they knew many of them would) they would go to heaven. Those two "hopes" made life bearable for them.

Those who have hope that they can make a difference in this life, and have hope of reward and eternal life after death, are able to face with joy the constant stream of diversions, disappointments, and defeats that life brings. Hope is a constant flow of water to a soul in the desert. Hope is a life jacket to a soul lost at sea. Hope is a pathway to one lost in the wilderness. The water, the life jacket, the pathway enable you to carry on, to put your confidence in the future.

If you have the hope that heaven is your place of reward, it might strengthen you to stick it out in a difficult marriage. It may strengthen you to be more honest and ethical in your business, even though it costs you money and the standard of living you hoped to have in this world. It may strengthen you to try to help others even if you are in poor health, or in poverty, or experiencing discrimination.

> **True hope strengthens us by truly resting on God's promise.**

When you have hope that this world is not your home, and that the true payoff for Christians will never be in this world, but in the next, it can strengthen you to be content in this world, even though this world has disappointed you.

When a church hopes, it places its confidence in the promises of God. It places its hope in the glory that is to be revealed to us at the coming of Jesus (Romans 8:18). It places its hope in the things that are not seen, rather than the things that are seen, for the things that are seen are temporary, but the things that are unseen are eternal (2 Corinthians 4:16–18).

The church that hopes endures the pain, the frustration, the lure of sin, the unfulfilled desires, the unanswered prayer, the circumstances gone awry, and remains faithful to the Lord, knowing that the future is when all things are set right. The church that hopes knows that

the sufferings we have now are nothing compared to the great glory that will be given to us. Everything that God made is waiting with excitement for the time when God will show the world who his children are. The whole world wants very much for that to happen. Everything that God made was changed to become useless. This was not by its own wish. It happened because God wanted it. But there was this hope: that everything God made would be set free from ruin. There was hope that everything God made would have the freedom and glory that belong to God's children.

We know that everything God made has been waiting until now in pain, like a woman ready to give birth. Not only the world, but we also have been waiting with pain inside us. We have the Spirit as the first part of God's promise. So we are waiting for God to finish making us his own children. I mean we are waiting for our bodies to be made free. We were saved, and we have this hope. If we see what we are waiting for, then that is not really hope. People do not hope for something they already have. But we are hoping for something that we do not have yet. We are waiting for it patiently (Romans 8:18–25 NCV).

Yes, this is our hope—that someday, everything will be set right. The church that hopes takes to heart Paul's words in Colossians 3:1–3:

If then you were raised with Christ, seek those things which are above, where Christ is, sitting at the right hand of God. Set your mind on things above, not on things on the earth. For you died, and your life is hidden with Christ in God.

Hope takes us out of ourselves and puts us into Christ and eternal things. Hope puts its confidence in the future and spends its resources on things that last for eternity.

WHAT IS LOVE?

Love is the exercise of my will for the good of another.

Scripture has three different words that are all translated into English as "love." *Agape* (pronounced uh-gop'-ay) means the exercise of my will for the good of another. *Philos* means the love of friendship. The original language of the New Testament also has another word for love, *eros*, which means physical love. It is a limitation of the English language that we translate all three of these words as "love," since they have such different meanings and produce such disastrous consequences if mixed up.

We often think of love as a sweeping emotion, a deep feeling of affection for someone. However that concept comes from Hollywood, not from Scripture. Elvis used to sing that his girl needed to "be his" tonight! It was now or never, because his love wouldn't wait. That is not love. That is a tidal wave of hormones crashing on the beach of life! That is not the noble character trait to which the apostle calls the church. That is the carnal appetite of an alley cat.

Throughout the recent history of song, film, and literature, the emotional bonding that is part of *philos* love or the physical desire of *eros* love are substituted for the selfless character trait of *agape* love.

While the Scriptures never define *agape*, they do describe it in 1 Corinthians 13:4–7:

Love suffers long and is kind; love does not envy; love does not parade itself, is not puffed up; does not behave rudely, does not seek its own, is not provoked, thinks no evil; does not rejoice in iniquity, but rejoices in the truth; bears all things, believes all things, hopes all things, endures all things.

Do you want to know if you are truly loving? Ask yourself if you are patient (suffer long). Are you kind? Are you puffed up? Do you behave rudely? Do you seek your own? We can get a very clear picture very quickly whether or not we are "loving" in the biblical sense. This is a far cry from Elvis's demand to have his cravings satisfied *tonight!*

If there is strife in the church, someone is not loving. If there is conflict, if there is petty jealousy, if there are power struggles, if there are factions and cliques in the church, it is not a loving church.

Francis Schaeffer once wrote a booklet entitled *The Mark of a Christian*. I read it many years ago, but it made a lasting impression on me. The mark Schaeffer referred to was love. Shortly before Jesus was to be crucified, He met with His disciples in an upper room to prepare them for what was to come. Here, He told them what this mark was:

> Little children, I shall be with you a little while longer. You will seek Me; and as I said to the Jews, "Where I am going, you cannot come," so now I say to you. A new commandment I give to you, that you love one another; as I have loved you, that you also love one another. By this all will know that you are My disciples, if you have love for one another. (John 13:33–35)

The passage has a condition in it. All people would know that they were Jesus' disciples *if* they had love for one another. Jesus gave them a command to love one another, but that command could be violated. But if they violated it, and did not have love for one another, the outside world would have no reason to believe that they were Jesus' disciples. It is possible to be a Christian without showing the mark, but if we expect non-Christians to know that we are Christians, we must show the mark.

In the same booklet, Schaeffer went on to another event that occurred just a few minutes later. Jesus had finished talking with His disciples and had begun to pray to God the Father. In this prayer He said,

> [I pray] that they all may be one, as You, Father, are in Me, and I in You; that they also may be one in Us, that the world may believe that You sent Me. (John 17:21)

In this passage, Jesus was implying that unity among Christians is a powerful argument that Jesus was sent from God. If the world sees unity among Christians, it has a reason to believe that God sent Jesus. The opposite, by inference, would also be true. If non-Christians do not see unity among Christians, they have a reason to believe that Christ was not sent from God (*The Church at the End of the Twentieth Century*, 133–153).

A number of years ago, I read a survey taken of people who said that they were not Christians. The two most common reasons they said they were not Christians were that they doubted that Christ was God, and because of all the hypocrites in the church. There seemed to me to be a correlation. They did not believe that Christ's disciples were true disciples (all the hypocrites) and they doubted that Christ was God (Christ was sent from God). It seems possible to me that the two major reasons people say they do not become Christians are because of the failure of the church in its two primary responsibilities: love and unity, which are really the flip side of each other.

> True love unifies believers so outsiders see the truth of Jesus displayed.

Even if the church manifested love and unity perfectly, not everyone in the whole world would become a Christian. Even in the years following the resurrection of Christ in the book of Acts, when Christianity was, arguably, at its best, not everyone wanted to become a Christian. If someone does not want to become a Christian, he will be able to find plenty of excuses. Unbelief never has enough proof.

On the other hand, to the degree that the church manifests love and unity, it is able to evangelize from a stance of strength. To the degree that the church does not manifest love and unity, it evangelizes from a position of weakness, having to overcome some valid concerns before a person has a reason to believe that Christians are true disciples and that Jesus has been sent from God.

CONCLUSION

Just as an individual has a character, so an institution has a character. The question is, what should the character of the church be? The apostle Paul answers that question. The church should be characterized by corporate faith, corporate hope, and corporate love. These three characteristics embody what it means for a group of people to become corporately mature in Christ.

SPEED BUMP!

Slow down to be sure you have gotten the main points of this chapter.

Q1. What is faith?

A1. Faith is believing what God has said and *acting* accordingly.

Q2. What is hope?

A2. Hope is putting your confidence in the *future.*

Q3. What is love?

A3. Love is the exercise of my *will* for the good of another.

FILL IN THE BLANK

Q1. What is faith?

A1. Faith is believing what God has said and _____ accordingly.

Q2. What is hope?

A2. Hope is putting your confidence in the _____.

Q3. What is love?

A3. Love is the exercise of my _____ for the good of another.

FOR FURTHER THOUGHT AND DISCUSSION

1. How strong do you think churches as a whole in the United States are in the areas of faith, hope, and love?

2. Have you known of churches that were strong in one or more of these traits? How did they manifest their strength?

3. What do you think is the greatest hindrance to a church exercising strong faith? Hope? Love?

4. If your church as a whole had your character as a person, how healthy would the church be? How strong would its faith, hope, and love be? What changes would it need to make?

WHAT IF I DON'T BELIEVE?

If I don't believe that these character traits are important for churches to possess, then I will probably not be very helpful to the church in these areas. In fact, if I do not think they are important for a church, I probably do not think they are important for me, and I am potentially one who contributes to the need for a character change in my own church.

FOR FURTHER STUDY

1. Scripture

- John 13:33–35
- Romans 8:18–25
- 1 Corinthians 13:13
- James 2:17

2. Books

Several other books are very helpful in studying this subject further. They are listed below in general order of difficulty. If I could read only one of these, I would read the first one.

The Walk, Gene Getz

The Church at the End of the Twentieth Century, Francis Schaeffer

4

WHAT IS THE CHURCH SUPPOSED TO DO? (PART ONE)

WORSHIP

> *A good shoe is a shoe you don't notice. Good reading becomes possible when you need not consciously think about eyes, or light, or print, or spelling. The perfect church service would be one we were almost unaware of; our attention would have been on God.*
> —C. S. Lewis

We know what many things are supposed to do.

- An army is supposed to fight.
- A band is supposed to play.
- A ballerina is supposed to pirouette.
- A school is supposed to educate and train.
- A baseball player is supposed to run, throw, and hit.
- A doctor is supposed to diagnose, prescribe, and heal.
- A flower is supposed to grow, bloom, and produce seeds.
- A farmer is supposed to plant, fertilize, weed, and harvest.
- A baby is supposed to eat, sleep, make noise, and spit up.
- A dog is supposed to eat, sleep, make noise, and spit up.

But what is a church supposed to do? Many of us could run through a list of things our church is currently doing, but is that what the church is *supposed* to do? And is that *everything* the church is supposed to do?

When you look at some churches, you get the feeling you ought to gear everything around evangelizing. When you look at other churches, you get the feeling you ought to build a beautiful sanctuary and worship God. When you look at other churches, you get the feeling you ought to get an overhead projector and study your Bible.

Then there are fads that hit the church like snowstorms in the Rockies. One decade, everyone is buying busses and picking up hundreds of children in the neighborhood. Another decade, everyone is starting twelve-step support groups. Another decade, everyone is getting a band and having seeker-sensitive worship services. Are these things right or wrong? Are they complete or partial? Are they temporal or eternal? When something new comes down the pike, should we do it or pass it up? How do you know? What should the church do, and how do we know we should do it?

These are enormous questions, but Scripture gives us some help in answering them. There is a key passage in the book of Acts that will give us some guidance. Let me set the stage for it. Jesus had made it clear during His lifetime that He was going to be crucified and resurrected. He said that He would build His church and the gates of hell would not prevail against it (Matthew 16:18). He gave His disciples clear instructions to "Go therefore and make disciples of all the nations, baptizing them in the name of the Father and of the Son and of the Holy Spirit, teaching them to observe all things that I have commanded you" (Matthew 28:19–20).

After He ascended into heaven, the disciples were to wait in Jerusalem until they were empowered with the Holy Spirit. Then they were to be witnesses to Him in Jerusalem, Judea, Samaria (the outlying provinces), and the uttermost parts of the world. They received the Holy Spirit on the day of Pentecost in Acts 2, and shortly afterward, many thousands of people became Christians. As soon as they did, they had to get organized, and did so by starting local churches. In Acts 2, we see the description of their activities, and can get some idea of what the church is supposed to do by analyzing what the first church did.

> So then, those who had received his word were baptized; and that day there were added about three thousand souls. They were continually devoting themselves to the apostles' teaching and to fellowship, to the breaking of bread and to prayer. Everyone kept feeling a sense of awe; and many wonders and signs were taking place

IN THIS CHAPTER WE LEARN THAT . . .

1. The church should worship because we are instructed to worship and because the example of the early church teaches us to worship.

2. To worship means to prostrate oneself before God.

3. We should worship in a way that is culturally relevant without violating any principle in Scripture.

4. Worshipers are the "actors" in worship and God is the audience.

5. Our worship should include a dual focus on the greatness and the nearness of God.

through the apostles. And all those who had believed were together and had all things in common; and they began selling their property and possessions and were sharing them with all, as anyone might have need. Day by day continuing with one mind in the temple, and breaking bread from house to house, they were taking their meals together with gladness and sincerity of heart, praising God and having favor with all the people. And the Lord was adding to their number day by day those who were being saved. (41–47 NASB)

Hidden within this description of what the first church did are clues as to what we ought to be doing today. Not all Christians agree about some things in this passage, but we will look at the ones upon which there is agreement.

WHY SHOULD THE CHURCH WORSHIP?

The church should worship because we are instructed to worship and because the example of the early church teaches us to worship.

Luke wrote in Acts 2 that the first Christians were "continually devoting themselves to the apostles' teaching and to fellowship, to the breaking of bread and to prayer" (v. 42). Then he said that "everyone kept feeling a sense of awe" (v. 43) and that they were "praising God" (v. 47). These things are at the heart of corporate worship. The phrase "continually devoting themselves" suggests single-minded faithfulness. Apparently when these first Christians got together for worship they were serious about it.

The phrase "kept feeling a sense of awe" could be translated, "fear came upon every soul." It does not mean "fear" in the sense of being frightened of someone. Rather, it means "awe" or "reverence" or "deep respect." These people had been deeply impressed with the presence of God and His work in their midst. It showed.

However, they were not prune-faced religious Scrooges whose very presence dumped a cloud of gloom on others. Verse 46 says that "gladness" characterized their activities, and they favorably impressed all those who saw them.

WHAT DOES IT MEAN TO WORSHIP?

To worship means to prostrate oneself before God.

In another book in this series, *What You Need to Know about God*, I discuss what it means to worship. Allow me to borrow that discussion for our purposes in this chapter:

Several Hebrew and Greek words in the Bible are translated "worship." But there is only one main Hebrew word for "worship" in the Old Testament and one main Greek word for "worship" in the New Testament. Both mean the same thing. Yet it does not mean "to sing," or "to gather together in a congregation," or "going through a ceremony," or even "to get quiet and solemn." The word "to worship" means, literally, "to prostrate oneself, to fall down on one's face."

I admit I was surprised by that. I don't think the word must always be taken literally. I don't think it must mean literally to fall down on one's face, though it can mean that. But it can also mean, in a figurative sense, to spiritually prostrate oneself before God.

> To worship means to offer ourselves completely to God.

Does that puzzle you, as it did me? What is intended by a word that means "to prostrate oneself"? When we prostrate ourselves figuratively before God, what are we doing? If we don't understand that we may not know what it means to worship.

Let's imagine what would be going on in our hearts and minds if we prostrated ourselves before someone else. If I prostrated myself before someone, I would be recognizing his authority. I would be affirming his superiority. I would be demonstrating my submission. I would be placing myself at his mercy and his disposal. It would be a massive gesture of total personal offering and sacrifice. In the land of the free and the home of the brave, in the land where all men are equal, in the land of rugged individualism, we can hardly imagine prostrating ourselves like that. But if we did, we would be saying, by our body language, "You are greater than we are, and we recognize that. We humble ourselves before You, place ourselves at Your mercy and disposal, and agree to do anything You tell us to do." Here is an act of total sacrifice.

So, when the Bible uses the word "worship" it means more than we may have thought. In John 4:23–24, we read, "An hour is coming, and now is, when the true worshipers shall worship the Father in spirit and truth; for such people the Father seeks to be His worshipers. God is spirit, and those who worship Him must worship in spirit and truth" (NASB). To paraphrase, God seeks people who will give themselves to Him totally. He is seeking people who will say, "You are greater than I am, and I recognize that. I humble myself to You, I place myself at Your mercy and disposal, and I agree to do anything You tell me to do."

Is that what you do on Sunday mornings? Worship, in its fundamental meaning, is an offering of the complete self to God. Unless we understand that, we will misunderstand both what *we* do in worship, and what *God* requires. As a result, we will miss the deep and meaningful relationship with God that we all long for. (167–168)

HOW SHOULD WE WORSHIP?

We should worship in a way that is culturally relevant
without violating any principle in Scripture.

So, one thing the first churches did was to worship God intensely, but with contagious joy. There are several scriptures that give us additional insight into biblical worship. For example, David made it clear that our worship could be enthusiastic and joyful. Psalm 100 says,

> Make a joyful shout to the LORD, all you lands!
> Serve the LORD with gladness;
> Come before His presence with singing.
> Know that the LORD, He is God;
> It is He who has made us, and not we ourselves;
> We are His people and the sheep of His pasture.
> Enter into His gates with thanksgiving,
> And into His courts with praise.
> Be thankful to Him, and bless His name.
> For the LORD is good;
> His mercy is everlasting,
> And His truth endures to all generations.

This is no picture of somber dirges being groaned out by stone-faced corpses who died long ago but have not had the decency to stop breathing. No, this is a picture of life! This is a picture of joy! This is a picture of uninhibited praise to God for who He is and what He has done!

When we look at Nehemiah, we see another example of a worship service. And what a service it was! The walls of Jerusalem had been destroyed and rebuilt. At the dedication ceremony of the new walls, Nehemiah, a leader of the Jewish people, planned a great time of worship and celebration.

They brought all the clergy to celebrate the dedication with gladness, both with thanksgivings and singing, with cymbals and stringed instruments and harps. Then Nehemiah brought all the leaders of Judah up on the wall that had been newly rebuilt. It must have been a huge wall, because he also appointed two large choirs that also went up on the wall. One choir walked one direction on the wall, presumably singing as they went, while another choir walked

> Worship celebrates who God is and what He has done with great freedom concerning how people may worship.

the other direction on the wall. At some point they met and went into the temple. The singers sang loudly, and the orchestra accompanied them. They offered great sacrifices and rejoiced, for God had made them rejoice with great joy; the women and the children also rejoiced, so that the joy of Jerusalem was heard afar off (paraphrased from Nehemiah 12:27–43). What a spectacle!

Not all worship services were done on such a grand scale, however; some were simple and quiet. On the night before Jesus was betrayed, for example, He met with His disciples in an upper room where they observed the Passover, during which time Jesus converted the observance of the Passover to the observance of the Lord's Supper, or communion (John 13—17). In addition to observing the first communion, they shared thoughts from Scripture, prayed, and sang hymns. There was no orchestra, no choir, no procession, no formal service, but there was worship.

So we see from the scriptural examples that there is great freedom in *how* we worship. But we are to worship.

WHO IS THE AUDIENCE IN WORSHIP?

Worshipers are the "actors" in worship, and God is the audience.

One problem many people face is that they are not able to find a church they are happy with. It seems that all the great churches are a thousand miles away. Not everyone has this problem, of course, but it is very common. Many people respond by not going to church, or by going but crabbing about things.

WHY I NEED TO KNOW THIS

Worship is not always easy. Sometimes we don't feel like worshiping. Sometimes we cannot find a church that we like. Other times, we don't know if the way our church is worshiping is okay in God's eyes. Because worship is not always easy, it requires a commitment to worship and a willingness to look for the best church we can find and try to make it better. Also, if we do not understand how to worship, we may go through the motions, but true worship is not happening. The better we understand worship, the more likely we are to be faithful and find it satisfying.

I don't want to minimize the frustration of this. My wife and I have been in that situation, and it is not as enjoyable as having a church that is a pleasure to attend. However, when we understand what worship is, we realize that we can worship even if the church does not do things the way we think they should be done.

Many of us have the idea that it is the church's responsibility to put on a good show that we enjoy, that moves us emotionally, and that we feel comfortable with. We see the ministers, the special music, the choir and instrumentalists as the actors on a stage, with ourselves as the audience. If the show is good, we reward the actors with our approval, presence, and financial support. If the show isn't so good, we may reduce our response. God is around somewhere, but we're not completely sure how He fits in. For many years, this was my concept of worship.

> We worship God because He is worthy, not in order to demand some experience in return.

However, true worship must be seen as a responsibility of each person in the pew. When worship is understood correctly, each person in the pew is seen as one of the "actors" too, *along with* the special music, the choir and instrumentalists, and the ministers, who are merely prompters and leaders. God Himself is the audience.

God wants us to worship Him, and we can do so, even if the ministers and musicians aren't as much help as we would like. Assuming that the ministers and musicians are not doing something offensive to God, we can worship. If we direct our thoughts to God and *mean* everything that is said, sung, and prayed, then we will worship.

I remember one time worshiping in a large, beautiful cathedral with granite walls, stained-glass windows, solid wood pews, and a gilded altar. The ceremony was a very old liturgy. I had reason to believe, because of what the minister had said and written, and by the lifestyles of many people in the church, that not everyone meant what they were saying in that ancient liturgy. But they could not keep me from meaning it. I remember worshiping deeply. I would have been happier if everyone there had meant what was said, sung, and prayed, and I doubt if I could have made that church my home, because it was very liberal theologically. But on that Sunday morning, I worshiped regardless of what anyone else did.

Worship is not an emotion (John 4:23–24). Rather, it is an offering to God. We offer God our praise, our prayers, our public declaration of the greatness of His person and His work. Sometimes worship will stir us emotionally, and sometimes it will not. In a worship service we primarily give something to God, and secondarily we receive something for ourselves. We worship God because He is deserving of our worship, not because we demand to get something out of the worship experience.

We must find the best church we can, and make a commitment to it, and try to help make it a better church. If we cannot find a church because there is something offensive to God about all the churches available for us to attend, or if there are other reasons, then we might have to consider helping start another one, even if it is only a meeting in a home with a few like-minded families. In the early days of the New Testament, and in some countries of the world today where there are few Christians, or where Christianity is outlawed, that is the way Christians worship. We can too.

WHAT SHOULD OUR FOCUS BE IN WORSHIP?

Our worship should include a dual focus on the greatness and the nearness of God.

The son of a king has to look at his father in two different ways. He is both a subject and a child, so he must look at his father both as his king and as his father. As a subject, the child is required to obey the laws of the land and be subject to the authority of the king. As a child, however, he has a closeness and a relationship that go beyond mere citizenship. He is able to crawl up in his lap and call him daddy.

So it is with us and God. God is our King, and God is our Father. As our King, we must obey and respect Him. As our Father, we are free to call Him "Daddy" (which is what "Abba" means in Romans 8:15).

These two different facets of our relationship to God affect our worship of Him. Sometimes in our worship we call attention to God our King. Other times, we may call attention to Jesus our Savior. Sometimes we focus on the greatness of God, and other times we may focus on the love of Jesus. Sometimes we highlight how far above us God is, and other times we may highlight how close Jesus is. One is not wrong and the other right. Rather, they are both aspects of our relationship with God, and it is legitimate, and even important, for us to balance our worship between these two facets of our relationship with God.

Some songs, some worship services, some churches, and even some denominations may tend to highlight one of the aspects more than the other. The song "A Mighty Fortress Is Our God," by the fiery reformer Martin Luther, focuses on the greatness and distance of God. The little chorus "Jesus Is the Sweetest Name I Know" focuses on His love and nearness.

Sometimes not just one song but an entire worship service might focus on the greatness and majesty of God; at other times the entire service might focus on the love and nearness of Jesus. When a church's services typically focus on one or the other, this focus is often reflected in the architecture of the building. If the building is made of stone, with stained-glass windows, a formal altar, with the pulpit to the side, with a communion table and a cross in the center, usually that church tends to worship in a lofty, more formal style that highlights the greatness and majesty of God. If the church has cedar siding, warm-colored carpet, padded chairs instead of pews, and the pulpit in the center of a simple platform, usually that church worships in a manner that focuses on the nearness of Jesus.

It is even true that some denominations tend toward one emphasis or the other. Episcopalian, Lutheran, and Presbyterian churches have more churches with an emphasis on more formal worship marked by classic architecture in church buildings and the use of vestments, a printed order of worship from which worshipers read prayers and other responses, and very frequent participation in communion. The many different kinds of Baptist denominations often have more churches that worship informally, with a simpler service emphasizing preaching and teaching more than the elements just listed.

As I said, one way is not right and the other wrong. However, regardless of which tradition you feel most comfortable with, there is a danger. Because both are true—God *is* great and majestic and distant and far above us, as well as being loving and close and always with us—if we only communicate one perspective, we risk having a lopsided view of God. This lopsidedness comes not only because of what we say and do, but also because of what we don't say and don't do.

Healthy worship focuses on both God's greatness and His nearness.

Through all our worship, we give praise to God for His grace and mercy to us. The apostle Paul wrote, "For by grace you have been saved through faith, and that not of yourselves; it is the gift of God, not of works, lest anyone should boast" (Ephesians 2:8–9). Not because of who we are, but because of who He is, He allows us to be adopted into His family, and He treats us like His beloved children for eternity.

For example, if our church has a formal cathedral with high granite walls, elaborate stained-glass windows, a pipe organ, a formal altar with a communion table and cross or crucifix at the center, many religious symbols, and a formal, liturgical style of worship service, then it will be clear to the congregation that God is all-powerful, all-knowing, everywhere present, majestic, and higher than we are. However, we are in danger of never helping our people understand that God is also near, loving, merciful, and kind.

On the other hand, if we have a simple wooden building with simple furniture, a plain platform with a lectern in the middle and no religious symbols, a piano and perhaps a worship band, with an informal worship service emphasizing preaching and teaching with no liturgy, then it will be clear to the congregation that Jesus is loving, merciful, kind, near, and always with us. However, we will be in danger of never helping our people understand that God is all-powerful, all-knowing, everywhere present, majestic, and higher than we are.

The tendency to prefer one of these focuses on God gives rise to traditional differences in worship service styles. Since the Bible does not tell us how to worship, we are free to adjust the worship style to fit the history and culture in which we live. To try to force charismatics in parts of Africa to sit in hard wooden pews and sing tightly controlled classical songs to an organ is likely to seem a little unnatural to them. On the other hand, to encourage Episcopalians in Boston to dress in colorful, informal garb and stand around in a circle outdoors, hopping up and down, chanting simple, repetitive songs while drums beat in the background would be possibly even more unnatural.

Is one right and the other wrong? Not necessarily. Any general worship style can be abused, or it can be made appropriate, depending on the spirit and truth being presented. In the United States, there are several different styles of worship.

1. Formal. The formal style emphasizes the recital of ancient creeds, the observance of communion, standardized formal prayers, readings from prayer books, and formal music with piano and organ.

2. Informal. The informal style emphasizes a more spontaneous worship style. Singing modern hymns and choruses, sometimes accompanied by a small band as well as piano and organ, is often a characteristic. In larger informal churches an orchestra is sometimes used. Occasionally, children are included in all or part of the service, even to the point of having a children's sermon before the adult sermon. More time is given to preaching than in the formal service, and a greater emphasis is often placed on public corporate evangelism.

3. Educational. A strong emphasis on teaching is a characteristic of some churches that may be formal or informal. A nationally known pastor in Florida has a formal, cathedral-style building, with pipe organ and formal altar with communion rail and a large cross. The music is more formal, employing a piano or pipe organ as standard accompaniment, but using some brass, string, or woodwind instruments to supplement from time to time. However, he is a very strong teacher and gives much more time to preaching than most formal churches do. Often, the churches that emphasize strong teaching in their worship style are less formal.

No one of these styles is right or wrong. No one church is right for everyone. The needs, interests, tastes, background, and temperaments of people are what create the different worship styles. If someone has a preference for one style, but finds himself in a church that emphasizes another style, he should not view his church as being in the wrong. Rather, he should recognize that the majority of people in that church have apparently preferred the present worship style. He might be advised to either accept the worship style or else change churches, rather than mount a one-man crusade to get the church to change to his viewpoint.

CONCLUSION

Scripture makes it clear that Christians are to worship God, but great freedom appears to be given to people to worship in whatever manner is most meaningful to them. There are certain principles that are to be followed in worship. We are to worship in spirit and in truth, which means that we are not to tolerate hypocrisy or meaninglessness in our worship (John 4:23). And the apostle Paul tells us that everything is to be conducted properly and in an orderly manner (1 Corinthians 14:40). But within these general guidelines, we are free to use whatever style most clearly expresses the heart of any given group of believers. However, when we ask the question, "What is the church supposed to do?" as we did in the opening of this chapter, worship is only one of the things a church is to do. We will explore other things in the next chapter.

SPEED BUMP!

Slow down to be sure you have gotten the main points of this chapter.

Q1. Why should the church worship?

A1. The church should worship because we are *instructed* to worship and because the *example* of the early church teaches us to worship.

Q2. What does it mean to worship?

A2. To worship means to *prostrate* oneself before God.

Q3. How should we worship?

A3. We should worship in a way that is culturally *relevant* without violating any principle in Scripture.

Q4. Who is the audience in worship?

A4. Worshipers are the "actors" in worship and *God* is the audience.

Q5. What should our focus be in worship?

A5. Our worship should include a *dual* focus on the greatness and the nearness of God.

FILL IN THE BLANK

Q1. Why should the church worship?

A1. The church should worship because we are _____ to worship and because the_____ of the early church teaches us to worship.

Q2. What does it mean to worship?

A2. To worship means to _____ oneself before God.

Q3. How should we worship?

A3. We should worship in a way that is culturally _____ without violating any principle in Scripture.

Q4. Who is the audience in worship?

A4. Worshipers are the "actors" in worship and _____ is the audience.

Q5. What should our focus be in worship?

A5. Our worship should include a _____ focus on the greatness and the nearness of God.

FOR FURTHER THOUGHT AND DISCUSSION

1. What are some of the most important specific ways that we can "prostrate" ourselves before God?

2. Do you think there are any ways that churches today violate scriptural principles in an attempt to be culturally relevant?

3. How do you think it will affect your personal worship if you keep in mind that you are an "actor" and God is the audience in worship?

4. Is your personal inclination to focus on the greatness or the nearness of God? How does that affect your worship? What do you think you could do to balance

yourself? What focus does your church tend to have? What could it do to balance itself?

WHAT IF I DON'T BELIEVE?

1. If I don't believe that participation in corporate worship is an obligation, I will probably not be as faithful to Sunday morning church attendance as I would otherwise be.
2. I will probably not be as willing to "hang in there" when the best church I can find still does not meet my hopes and expectations.
3. If I don't realize that differences in worship style that don't violate biblical principles are natural and acceptable, I may not be tolerant of others who do not hold my preferences.

4. If I don't understand that God is the audience in a worship service and I attend a church because, overall, it is the best church available to me, even though it does not share my preferences in worship style, I may fall into the trap of attending the church, but not really supporting it spiritually, emotionally, or financially. I may be a critical church member, and we have too many of those.

FOR FURTHER STUDY

1. Scripture

- Nehemiah 12:27–43
- Psalm 100
- Matthew 16:18
- Matthew 28:19–20
- John 4:23
- John 13–17
- Acts 2:42–47

2. Books

Several other books are very helpful in studying this subject further. They are listed below in general order of difficulty. If I could read only one of these, I would read the first one.

Up with Worship, Anne Ortlund

The Bride, Charles Swindoll

What You Need to Know about God, Max Anders

5

WHAT IS THE CHURCH SUPPOSED TO DO? (PART TWO)

INSTRUCTION, FELLOWSHIP, AND MINISTRY

When I first became a Christian, about fourteen years ago, I thought that I could do it on my own, by retiring to my rooms and reading theology, and I wouldn't go to the churches and gospel halls . . . I disliked very much their hymns, which I considered to be fifth-rate poems set to sixth-rate music. But as I went on I saw the great merit of it.
—C. S. Lewis

I once read (I don't remember where) that James Earl Jones, that actor with thunder in his voice, wrote a poem for school when he was a young boy. It was a very good poem, and his teacher thought he had copied it. James protested, so the teacher said, "All right, if you wrote the poem, recite it to me." Jones recited it verbatim. The teacher was convinced, and went on to encourage Jones to expand his talents.

That story struck me, because I have written many poems, but I couldn't recite one of them if my life depended on it. I have a friend who is seventy-six and often recites poems and other things she learned as a child in school. There are some things I have memorized repeatedly and still can't remember them very well. If that incident had happened to me instead of James Earl Jones, I would probably still be sitting in the principal's office.

Knowledge is a tricky thing. It is hard to gain it initially and it is hard to keep it. I once heard the true story of a couple who, after a long and difficult labor, were blessed with their second child, a daughter beautiful and perfect in every way. Later, in the hospital room, the husband looked tenderly at the new little life in his arms with tears in his eyes. Then he glanced up at his wife, who expected him to utter something truly poetic. Instead, he asked, "What's her name again?"

Perhaps you've never done anything that bad, but how many times have you hit your head against a brick wall because you didn't know enough to solve a problem you were facing, or groped for something you used to know but could no longer remember? We all struggle with gaining enough knowledge and then retaining it.

And where is it any more difficult than in learning the Bible? Many of us are familiar with the stories of the Bible and vaguely familiar with some of the verses in the Bible. But just let us get into a conversation with someone about what the Bible says regarding a particular issue, and our mind goes blank. It is as though we had never read the Bible.

Our problem goes back to something Solomon said in Proverbs 22:17–19: "Incline your ear and hear the words of the wise, and apply your mind to my knowledge; for it will be pleasant if you keep them within you, that they may be ready on your lips" (NASB).

Ah, there's the trick. Most of us have only become generally familiar with the Bible, but Solomon says that we should study the Bible well enough that the information will be "ready on our lips." That is, we should know the Bible well enough that we can remember it and talk about the information. Using that measure, many of us do not know the Bible well enough.

Jesus was the perfect example of knowing the Bible well enough to use it like a spiritual laser beam. In Matthew 4, after His baptism by John the Baptist in the Jordan River, Jesus went out into the wilderness where He fasted for forty days and nights. Then Satan came to Him to tempt Him to sin, hoping that He would not begin His ministry as the Messiah. Satan tempted Jesus three times, and each time Jesus quoted a passage of Scripture in His defense. For example, Satan said, knowing that Jesus would be extremely hungry, "If you are the Son of God, command that these stones become bread." But Jesus answered him and said, "It is written, 'Man shall not live by bread alone, but by every word that proceeds from the mouth of God'" (vv. 3–4).

IN THIS CHAPTER WE LEARN THAT . . .

1. The church should teach the Scriptures to help people master the Bible well enough to mature spiritually.

2. The church should promote fellowship because Christians need each other for support to live the Christian life.

3. The church must minister because of the needs of Christians within the church as well as the needs of those outside the church.

If, when we are tempted to sin, we could remember a Scripture passage that specifically addressed the issue we were facing, we would find it much easier to withstand the temptation. For example, when we are tempted to watch something on television that we ought not to watch, if we knew Philippians 4:8 well enough, its words would pop into our minds:

Whatever is true, whatever is honorable, whatever is right, whatever is pure, whatever is lovely, whatever is of good repute, if there is any excellence and if anything worthy of praise, dwell on these things. (NASB)

It would be very difficult to have this verse in your mind and watch most television at the same time. That is how Scripture becomes most valuable, when you know it so well that specific verses come to your mind in life's situations. This will only happen as we become serious and dedicated students of the Bible.

WHY SHOULD THE CHURCH TEACH THE SCRIPTURES?

The church should teach the Scriptures to help people
master the Bible well enough to mature spiritually.

A church that only sings and offers prayer to God is like a ship that has a sail but no rudder. Yes, it is going somewhere, but is it going to the right place? Truth is foundational to Christianity. Jesus said, "You shall know the truth, and the truth shall make you free" (John 8:32). An expressive, exuberant Christianity is not sufficient. Everything we do must be rooted in the truth. Again, Jesus said, "Sanctify them by Your truth. Your word is truth" (John 17:17). If we are to grow spiritually we must be grounded in the truth, in the Word of God. That is why we read, in

> **Exuberant worship without the ministry of the Word makes a church be like a ship with a sail but no rudder.**

Acts 2:42, "and they continued steadfastly in the apostles' doctrine." Without the foundation of biblical instruction, Christians will not mature spiritually, and neither will the church, corporately.

In 2 Timothy 3:16–17 the apostle Paul wrote,

All Scripture is given by inspiration of God, and is profitable for doctrine, for reproof, for correction, for instruction in righteousness, that the man of God may be complete, thoroughly equipped for every good work.

If we want to be complete (which means "mature"), and if we want to be equipped for every good work, we must depend on the Scripture. We must be founded and rooted in the truth of the Word. Everything the Christian should know, should become, should do is based in the Scripture. Not that we ignore anything that is not in the Bible (2 + 2 = 4 is true, but is not in the Bible), but that we evaluate everything outside the Bible by what the Bible says. A high view of Scripture, which must include a deep commitment to mastering its teachings and allowing its teachings to master us, is essential to all that God wants for His children.

If this is true, then the church must instruct its people in the truth, and we see that the first church did. "They continued steadfastly in the apostles' doctrine [or teaching]" (v. 42). What was the apostles' doctrine? We don't know for sure, but it would have included everything that Jesus taught. Much of this would be found in the Gospels, but surely not all the apostles heard Him teach in the three years they spent with Him was recorded in the Gospels. In addition, it would have included their teaching of the crucifixion, resurrection, and ascension of our Lord, as well as His charge to go into all the world and preach the gospel.

WHY I NEED TO KNOW THIS

If I am going to live a balanced life myself, if I am going to be able to choose wisely a church to attend, and if I am going to be able to help make my church a better church, I need to know what the responsibilities of the church are. Otherwise, I suffer, the church suffers, and those we might have helped suffer.

So, whatever the apostles taught, the first church continued steadfastly in it. We see the importance that the early church placed on the truth when, in Acts 6, a complaint arose among some of the Jews that, as they lived in a temporary communal condition, some of the widows and orphans were being overlooked in the daily distribution of food. They wanted the apostles to fix the problem.

Indirectly, they did. They said, "Seek out from among you seven men of good reputation, full of the Holy Spirit and wisdom, whom we may appoint over this business; but we will give ourselves continually to prayer and to the ministry of the word" (vv. 3–4). The study and teaching of the Word was of such priority that they would let nothing keep them from the responsibility.

If we are to maintain the priorities of the New Testament church, we must place a powerful priority on the preaching of and instruction in the Word of God. It is not enough to be vaguely familiar with the stories of the Bible. We must know the spiritual principles and truths so well that we are able to guide and order our daily lives and continuous thoughts after the truth of the Word. If a person or a church is not well instructed in the Scriptures, they are easy prey to false teaching, to discouragement, to imbalance, to wrong steps taken in ignorance, and to forgetfulness. If you want healthy sheep, the shepherd must make sure they are well fed. So a second priority for any church, after worship, is instruction in the Word.

Instruction must be kept in balance. Just as vegetables are good for you, and essential to overall health, if you eat nothing but vegetables, you will not be healthy. You must balance vegetables with other things for a complete diet. The same is true with instruction. We must stress the critical importance of biblical instruction, but in doing so, we must never give the impression that instruction is all there is.

When I was in seminary, a group of single guys in my dorm did not go to church on Sunday morning. Instead, they met together in one of their rooms and listened to a tape of their pastor back home. He was a teacher of the Word! He, and he alone, seemed to be able to discern the truth from Scripture, so no one else was worth listening to. Neither was it important to worship corporately. Neither was it important to reach out to the lost or the disadvantaged or to take communion. The church service back home was a quick hymn (to let people know they should sit down and be quiet), a quick offering (somebody's got to pay for this building and these salaries), and fifty minutes of deep Bible teaching complete with the original languages and an overhead projector. So they approximated that service by getting together, listening to a tape, and calling it a day.

> **A church that only instructs people in the Word is like a ship with a huge rudder but no sail.**

As crucial as good instruction is, it is only part of what a Christian needs, and only part of what a church should do. A church that studies so hard that it does nothing else is like a ship with a huge rudder but no sail. If it ever got any wind, it might know exactly, precisely where to go. But there is no sail, no life, no energy. If you want to get someplace in a sailboat, you must have both rudder and sail.

WHY SHOULD THE CHURCH PROMOTE FELLOWSHIP?

The church should promote fellowship because Christians need each other for support to live the Christian life.

Look at the description of the Christians in the first church in Acts 2. They "continued in fellowship"; they "were together." They took care of each other, whenever anyone had need. They continued "with one accord"; they "broke bread from house to house." They lived as part of each other's lives.

There appear to be two issues involved in the matter of fellowship. First is the fact that they spent time with each other, enjoyed each other, and drew strength from each other. We are becoming more and more isolated. In the not-too-distant past, our houses had front porches where people sat and visited when they had the time. Now, we have back patios with fences around them. We used to leave our doors unlocked. Now, we barricade ourselves behind iron bars and security systems. We used to visit with others when we had the chance. Now we turn on the television. We are becoming more and more isolated.

It affects even those in the church. We tend to be so busy that if anyone drops by unexpectedly, it interrupts us from something important. We do not have the normal communal life that used to be part of American culture. Yes, there are enough problem people out there that we cannot turn the clock back. But as a result, we have developed a living pattern of isolation that not only protects us from dangerous people, but also cuts us off from the very people we need in order to live a balanced and healthy life.

The image of a body was well chosen by Jesus to "picture" the collection of Christians called the "church." A body has many different members, very unlike each other, yet when they fit together, they form a "whole" that works quite well. What would you do if, next Sunday in church, an eyeball came rolling up to you and said, "Hi"? Doubtless, it would unnerve you!

Christians were never intended to function alone.

As bizarre an image as that creates on a physical level, it is no more bizarre than a lone Christian on a spiritual level trying to be everything to himself. A Christian was never intended to function alone spiritually, any more than an eyeball was intended to function alone physically. God created Christians to be healthy only as they are in good relationship with other Christians. Solitary confinement in prison is one of the worst possible forms of punishment because people need other people. So if a church is going to function normally, if it is going to have biblical priorities, if it is going to have healthy members, it must encourage, promote, and champion fellowship.

The second issue is that they took care of each other. If anyone had a need, the group as a whole met it. Granted, this is a difficult challenge today. Many people today appear unwilling or unable to be responsible, to make hard decisions, and to sacrifice things today for a higher goal tomorrow. They are in financial trouble or legal trouble or interpersonal trouble because of their own poor decisions and behavior, yet they don't respond when given help. It is hard to know exactly what to do with these people. Sincere Christians want to help, but often don't know how without getting swallowed alive or merely aiding and abetting the other person's irresponsible behavior.

I know of very few churches, and almost no large churches, who are able to take care of each other the way the early church did, because there are too many irresponsible people attending the church. Not only should many of them not be encouraged in an irresponsible lifestyle, but also, the responsible ones do not have enough collective wealth to take care of all the irresponsible ones.

Trying to function like the early New Testament church in this regard is an overwhelming challenge. Perhaps more stringent requirements to receive assistance from a church might help us find a way to achieve a healthy balance in this matter.

The irresponsible people notwithstanding, one thing is certain. We should help people with legitimate needs. We cannot let the abusers of the system keep us from being sensitive to the needs of those who really need our help and would not abuse the system. Each local church must decide for itself how it will meet this mandate, but meet it we must. A small-group ministry in a church, like home groups, support groups, and other groups organized around common interests, is a way to break down larger churches into smaller units so that more individual needs can be met.

WHY MUST THE CHURCH MINISTER TO OTHERS?

The church must minister because of the needs of Christians within
the church as well as the needs of those outside the church.

The first church in Acts ministered very naturally, as an overflow of what God had done for them. The Holy Spirit had done some very remarkable things among the first Christians in Jerusalem, and thousands of people believed the powerful message preached by Peter on the day of Pentecost. These Christians then ministered to one another, fellowshiping, breaking bread together, and dividing possessions to meet one another's needs. But in addition to all that, they reached out to those who had not yet heard. They continued to visit the temple, presumably telling others about their experience, since "the Lord added to the church daily those who were being saved" (v. 47).

"People are not persuaded— they're attracted."

Of course, the church is given much more complete instructions later on in the New Testament regarding its ministry. The apostle Paul wrote in his letter to the Galatians, "Therefore, as we have opportunity, let us do good to all, especially to those who are of the household of faith" (Galatians 6:10). We minister to one another, and we minister to those who are not of the faith. This is the pattern we see in the first church.

In ministering to one another, there is the long list of "one anothers" that we find in chapter 1 of this volume. In addition, we are to minister with our spiritual gift to one another (Romans 12; 1 Corinthians 12; Ephesians 4:11–16).

In ministering to non-Christians, of course we are to evangelize them (Matthew 28:19–20). Later, in Acts 4, Peter was again preaching, and they were arrested, jailed, and warned not to preach the name of Jesus anymore. Of course they did. In chapter 5, we read that "every day" in the temple and from house to house, they kept right on teaching and preaching Jesus as the Christ (vv. 41–42).

In *The Bride*, Chuck Swindoll makes four observations about evangelism and outreach in the New Testament:

1. *[Evangelism] was never limited to a church gathering.* In fact, it occurred there least of all. The church gathered to be instructed and to worship. The church scattered to help, affirm, encourage, and evangelize. Today we often get it reversed. We think the church gathered ought to evangelize. The church can be thought of like a football team. They only huddle long enough to get the plays. Through the week, we run the plays.

2. *Evangelism was always initiated by the Christian.* We cannot assume that if someone wants to become a Christian, he will come up to us and ask. That rarely happens. So Christians initiate the contact.

3. *Evangelism was usually connected with another unrelated event or experience.* As the early Christians went about obeying Christ, it created opportunities for them to share their faith, and when they did, people came to Christ.

4. *Evangelism was never something anyone was forced into or manipulated to do.* Christians did not force themselves on non-Christians. Almost without exception, people were treated with tact and respect. The power of the ministry is the Holy Spirit. As He leads and we follow, caring for people, becoming interested in their world, their personal concerns, other people are attracted to Christ and want to hear our message. (59–60)

When Christians demonstrate love to one another, and a care and concern for others in general, it provides a powerful backdrop for evangelism, as we saw in chapter 3. In *Saints and Snobs*, Marion Jacobsen wrote of this connection between caring and evangelism:

If any group of Christians who claim to believe and practice all God has said in His Book will face up to their personal responsibility within the family of Christ, and to the real needs of Christians around them, their church will impress its community with the shining goodness of God's love—to them *and* among them. Such a transformation probably would do more to attract others to Jesus Christ than any house-to-house canvass, evangelistic campaign, or new church facility. People are hungry for acceptance, love, and friends, and unless they find them in the church they may not stay there long enough to become personally related to Jesus Christ (88).

People are not persuaded—they're attracted. We must be able to communicate far more by what we are than by what we say.

CONCLUSION

Certainly, the brief description of the events of the first church do not give us a complete picture of what the church today should do. But it does give us a fundamental picture. The early church worshiped God, giving Him not only their public praise and worship, but also their own lives in response to God's offer of salvation through Jesus. They taught themselves in the Word, using it as the foundational knowledge for faith and life. They fellowshiped, living in unity and harmony, caring for the physical, spiritual, and emotional needs of one another. And they ministered to one another and sought to evangelize the world. If this was their pattern in the earliest days, we might do more today, but we certainly ought not do less.

SPEED BUMP!

Slow down to be sure you have gotten the main points of this chapter.

Q1. Why should the church teach the Scriptures?

A1. The church should teach the Scriptures to help people master the Bible well enough to *mature* spiritually.

Q2. Why should the church promote fellowship?

A2. The church should promote fellowship because Christians need each other for *support* to live the Christian life.

Q3. Why must the church minister to others?

A3. The church must minister because of the *needs* of Christians within the church as well as the needs of those outside the church.

FILL IN THE BLANK

Q1. Why should the church teach the Scriptures?

A1. The church should teach the Scriptures to help people master the Bible well enough to_____ spiritually.

Q2. Why should the church promote fellowship?

A2. The church should promote fellowship because Christians need each other for_____to live the Christian life.

Q3. Why must the church minister to others?

A3. The church must minister because of the_____of Christians within the church as well as the needs of those outside the church.

FOR FURTHER THOUGHT AND DISCUSSION

1. How well does your church do in instructing its people in the Scriptures? What do you think could be done to improve this ministry? How good a Bible student are you? How well do you avail yourself of learning opportunities both within and outside your church?

2. How well does your church do in promoting true Christian fellowship? Do you fellowship with other Christians? How do you think you and your church might improve in this area?

3. How well does your church meet needs within and outside the church? What more could be done? How well do you personally respond to needs that come across your path?

WHAT IF I DON'T BELIEVE?

1. Since the Bible is so difficult to master, if I don't believe in the need for instruction, I am likely to remain biblically undereducated. As a result, I am liable to be continually frustrated in my Christian walk, since I will not know the Bible well enough to keep from "shooting myself in the foot," inflicting pain in my life that could have been avoided had I just known the Bible better.

2. If I don't believe in the need for fellowship, I am likely to be lonely and struggle in the Christian life, since God never intended for us to be able to make it alone. We need each other, and unless we live in fellowship with one another,

we cannot be deeply fulfilled in life, nor will we receive the help we need to live successfully.

3. If I don't believe in the need to minister to others, I will not invest the time and talents and treasures necessary to reach out to others. As a result, I will be spiritually stunted and will not experience the personal reward of being used significantly by God in the lives of others. In addition, I may not receive the help I need when I am in trouble.

FOR FURTHER STUDY

1. Scripture

- Matthew 4:1–11
- John 8:32
- John 17:17
- Romans 12
- 1 Corinthians 12
- Galatians 6:10
- Ephesians 4:11–16
- Philippians 4:8
- 2 Timothy 3:16–17

2. Book

The Bride, Charles Swindoll

6

WHO CAN LEAD THE CHURCH?

The church is looking for better methods;
God is looking for better men.
—E. M. Bounds

T he power of leadership is astonishing. I will never forget my sophomore year in high school. The Cold War between the United States and the Soviet Union had dropped to arctic conditions. Europe had allowed us to put nuclear weapons very near the Soviet border, so the Soviets wanted nuclear weapons near our border and started building nuclear missile sites in Cuba. When the evidence for this was incontrovertible, President Kennedy ordered a blockade of Cuba, so that the Soviets could not get the remaining materials into Cuba to complete the missile sites.

Premier Khrushchev ordered the Soviet ships that were steaming toward Cuba to violate the blockade. President Kennedy ordered our navy to intercept them. It was, perhaps, the most tense moment the world has ever known. Someone described it as looking down the nuclear gun barrel, wondering if it was going to go off.

I will never forget finishing basketball practice on the day before the Soviet ships were to arrive in Cuban waters. Instead of a riot of laughter and activity in the shower room after practice, we all sat down and talked about whether or not we thought there would be nuclear war. Would we be alive tomorrow at that same time? The world held its breath that night.

The next day, Kennedy repeated his ultimatum. The Soviet ships would be intercepted and the missile sites in Cuba dismantled or else! About midway through the day, I learned that Khrushchev had ordered the Soviet ships to turn around. The world breathed a sigh of relief. In the standoff, with the two nations staring down each other's nuclear gun barrels, the Soviets blinked.

The course of history was changed in just a few days through courageous leadership.

IN THIS CHAPTER WE LEARN THAT . . .

1. The Bible mentions pastor-teachers, elders, and deacons as the three leadership ministries of the church.
2. The basis of leadership in the church is spiritual maturity.

All great undertakings rely on great leadership. No great country ever arose without great statesmen. No great military victories were ever won without great generals. No great music was ever played without great composers. No great wealth was ever created without great entrepreneurs.

Just as great undertakings need great leadership, lesser undertakings need lesser leadership, but everything needs leadership. From nations, to states, to businesses, to families, to churches, everything needs leadership. The power of leadership in the church is just as great, and good leadership just as necessary, as in any other area. However, while leadership in many other areas depends on power, leadership in the church depends on spiritual maturity and a servant heart. To get a more complete picture of leadership in the church, we need to look more closely at some important questions.

WHAT ARE THE BIBLICAL POSITIONS OF CHURCH LEADERSHIP?

The Bible mentions pastor-teachers, elders, and deacons as
the three leadership ministries of the church.

There are three divinely ordained categories of leadership in the church: pastor-teachers, elders, and deacons.

Pastor-Teachers. Regarding pastor-teachers, in the early days of our country, the minister was often the best-educated person in town. He was the primary source of information, not only about the Bible but about the world. People gathered in church on Sunday morning with the same sense of expectation that we might turn on the news, or open up the newspaper or newsmagazine. Knowledge was power, and since the minister had much of the knowledge, he also had much of the power.

Today, however, knowledge is largely available to all who want or seek it. There are people in every congregation who know more about a given subject than the pastor. John might know more about politics than the pastor. Mary might know more about the arts. Bill might know more about business. Susan might know more about education. Henry might know more about finances. Harry might be a Christian family counselor, Jane a well-known Bible teacher, Lyle a church growth expert at a nearby seminary, and David a Greek teacher at the local university. If you add up John, Mary, Bill, Susan, Henry, Harry, Jane, Lyle, and David, the congregation, collectively, may know more than the pastor does.

Nevertheless, the pastor must pass two tests, and if he does, he is qualified to pastor. First, he must meet the spiritual-maturity qualifications for leadership established in 1 Timothy 3:1–7 and Titus 1:5–9, which we will look at in the next chapter. Second, he must possess the spiritual gift of pastor-teacher in Ephesians 4:11. If he possesses these two qualifications, he can be used by God to pastor a church, regardless of what everyone else in the congregation knows. Church leadership is essentially spiritual leadership by one who is divinely gifted for the task.

The ministry of pastor-teacher is not clearly articulated in Scripture. In fact, the only use of the term is found in Ephesians 4:11. The word *pastor* means "shepherd," and the word is used as "shepherd" elsewhere in the New Testament. The primary task of the pastor, in addition to the general responsibilities of shepherding the flock, is the "equipping of the saints for the work of ministry, for the edifying of the body of Christ" (Ephesians 4:12). Other than that general description, the function of the ministry is not described or defined.

WHY I NEED TO KNOW THIS

I need to know this because in choosing a church, I need to be sure it is following biblical patterns in its leadership positions, and I need to know that it takes the matter of spiritual maturity in its leaders seriously. Otherwise, I may put my spiritual life and the spiritual lives of those I care for in the hands of those who are not qualified to be responsible for them.

Not all are in agreement on the term "pastor-teacher." Ephesians 4:11 reads, "And He gave some as apostles, and some as prophets, and some as evangelists, and some as pastors and teachers" (NASB). Many people believe that there are five ministries described in this passage, and that is a credible position. However, there are factors unseen in the English text that give weight to the possibility that there are only four.

In Greek (the original language of the New Testament), the most common word for "and" is *kai*. However, there is another Greek word, *de*, usually translated "but," that is also often translated as "and." Both *kai* and *de* are used in this passage, and may lend weight to the interpretation. Also, the phrase "some as" occurs in front of apostles, prophets, evangelists, and pastors, but not in front of "teachers." In addition, the Greek has the word *the* in front of apostles, prophets, evangelists, and pastors, but not before "teachers." Keep these translations in mind as we re-read the passage with the original words in place:

"And He Himself gave some as *the* apostles, *kai* some as *the* prophets, *kai* some as *the* evangelists, *kai* some as *the* pastors *de* teachers."

So our task is to explain why the phrase "some as" and the word "the" come before only the first four words and not before "teachers," and why Paul changed from *kai* to *de* between the words "pastors" and "teachers." While there is room for responsible differences of opinion, a strong explanation is that there are not two, but only *one* gift being referred to: pastor-teacher. Seen this way, there is no such thing as a pastor. There is only a pastor-teacher, though for cultural reasons, I have no quarrel whatever with calling a person a "pastor" rather than the more cumbersome "pastor-teacher."

> Pastors must be spiritually mature and possess the gift of pastor-teacher.

Elders. The word for "elder" means to shepherd the congregation (1 Peter 5:2), to oversee its affairs, to preach and teach (1 Timothy 5:17), and to guard the moral purity of the congregation (Titus 1:9). An elder, just as a pastor-teacher, should also meet the spiritual maturity qualifications established in 1 Timothy 3:1–7 and Titus 1:5–9.

Deacon. A deacon's task is not as clearly defined in Scripture as an elder's. The word for "deacon" means "to serve," and a major use of the word for "deacon" has to do with waiting on tables. So, whatever a deacon is to do, it falls within the general category of serving. It is possible that the ministry of deacons was first seen in Acts 6:1–6, when widows and orphans were being overlooked in the daily distribution of food. So the church was instructed to choose men full of wisdom and of the Holy Spirit, and they were to oversee the proper distribution of food while the apostles devoted themselves to prayer and the ministry of the Word.

Whether or not deacons are supposed to be functioning in every church is not clear, but if a church chooses to have deacons, they must be spiritually mature. Their qualifications also clearly spelled out in 1 Timothy 3:8–13.

Questions. The ministry of an elder is not completely clear in the Bible. There is overlap between the responsibilities of elders and the responsibilities of pastor-teachers. Both are supposed to "shepherd" the church. Both, apparently, may preach and teach. Yet the pastor-teacher is responsible to equip the saints for the work of ministry. This could be implied in the responsibilities of an elder to preach and teach, but it could also be a distinct responsibility and gift of the pastor-teacher. This has led to differences of opinion about what an elder is.

1. Some believe that a pastor-teacher and an elder are two different positions, even though they are both called "shepherds." A pastor is one who is spiritually gifted to shepherd, but he is also spiritually gifted to teach. An elder must be *able* to shepherd and to teach, according to the qualifications listed in 1 Timothy and Titus, but is not spiritually gifted as a pastor-teacher. As a parallel example, all of us are supposed to evangelize, but not all of us have the gift of evangelism. In this way, perhaps, an elder is supposed to shepherd and teach, but he does not have the gift of pastor-teacher.

2. Some believe that a pastor-teacher and an elder are the same thing. Among those who hold this position, however, there are two different perspectives:

   a. Some believe that, since a pastor-teacher and an elder are the same thing, a church would only have one elder, who is the senior pastor.

   b. Others believe that the Bible teaches that each church should have more than one elder. Therefore if a church has multiple elders, they would also have multiple pastors. Every elder is a pastor-teacher and every pastor-teacher is an elder.

All of these positions are possible, and there are many thriving churches that operate under all three perspectives. The primary question to me seems to hinge on the issue of spiritual giftedness. In Ephesians 4:11, the apostle Paul makes it clear that four (or five) kinds of people have been spiritually gifted to play a crucial role in the life of the church: apostles, prophets, evangelists, and pastor-teachers. These are not people who aspire to these ministries or who merely volunteer for these ministries. These are people who are chosen and gifted by God for these ministries. They automatically perform these ministries because it is built into them by God. Cows moo, ducks quack, evangelists evangelize, and pastor-teachers pastor and teach. It is inherent within their makeup.

> **Elders must be spiritually mature, but they do not need to possess the pastor-teacher gift.**

Elders, on the other hand, apparently may simply *volunteer* for their ministry. The apostle Paul wrote in 1 Timothy 3:1, "If any man as*pires* to the office of overseer, it is a fine work he *desires* to do (NASB, emphasis added). So an elder may "aspire" to the ministry, which means "to have an ambition." If so, it is a fine work he *desires* to do, or wants to do. It seems that if a person simply wants to be an elder, he may, assuming he meets the qualifications.

However, I question if a person can merely *aspire* to the ministry of a pastor-teacher. An apostle could not merely aspire to his ministry. He was gifted and chosen by God for it. A prophet could not merely aspire to his ministry. He was gifted and chosen by God for it. An evangelist cannot merely aspire to his ministry. He must be gifted and chosen by God for it. So it seems to me that a person cannot merely aspire to the ministry of pastor-teacher. He must be gifted and chosen by God for the ministry.

If he has been spiritually gifted as a pastor-teacher, he is one, even though it may take time and training for him to actually be ready to take on the task. If a person has not been given the spiritual gift of pastor-teacher, no matter what he does, he will never be a pastor-teacher in the biblical sense.

A person who is spiritually gifted as a pastor-teacher may not be employed by a local church. But he will be pastoring and teaching wherever he is, no matter how he may be making a living. And, a person may be employed by a church as a pastor without having the spiritual gift of pastor-teacher. We might summarize the distinction by saying that a pastor-teacher is not merely something you do; it is something you are.

WHAT IS THE BASIS OF LEADERSHIP IN THE CHURCH?

The basis of leadership in the church is spiritual maturity.

Max DuPree, chairman of the Herman Miller Company, a large office furniture company, wrote that the first task of leadership is to define reality. And the last is to say thank you (*Leadership Is an Art*, 11). I think there is great insight in those statements. In the church, *spiritual maturity enables* you to define reality and *prompts* you to say thank you to those who helped pursue the goal.

Defining reality. The leader must know where he is, where he wants to go, and how he wants to get there. Spiritually, this can only be done by the mature. Spiritually immature people are easily deceived at best, and are carnal at worst (2 Timothy 2:24–26; James 3:13–18). Unless a leader in the church is spiritually mature, he cannot fully be trusted, and his decisions cannot fully be trusted.

Saying thank you. In Mark 10, Jesus and His twelve disciples were walking on the road to Jerusalem when James and John sidled up next to Him and said, "Teacher, we want You to do for us whatever we ask." It is hard to imagine two grown men thinking Jesus would fall for that, and He didn't.

"What do you want Me to do for you?" He asked.

They said to Him, "Grant us that we may sit, one on Your right hand and the other on Your left, in Your glory."

Jesus said that He was not able to grant that request, that the Father was the one to determine that.

The other disciples overheard this little power grab and got royally bent out of shape. But Jesus called them to Himself and said to them, "You know that those who are considered rulers over the Gentiles lord it over them, and their great ones exercise authority over them. Yet it shall not be so among you; but whoever desires to become great among you shall be your servant. And whoever of you desires to be first shall be slave of all. For even the Son of Man did not come to be served, but to serve, and to give His life a ransom for many" (vv. 35–45 summarized).

> **Christian leaders are called to discern and help meet spiritual needs.**

This exchange between Jesus and His disciples is a landmark passage defining how leadership is to function in the church. Leaders are to serve. It should be the goal of Christian leaders to discern the needs of those they are leading and find the best ways to meet those needs.

This does not mean that leaders are human vending machines, obligated to dispense whatever anyone asks for. That would be impossible. If you are a pastor, John might come up to you and say, "Pastor, I want to sing only praise choruses in church on Sunday," while Elizabeth might ask the next day that only hymns from the hymnal be sung. No, the servant leader cannot meet everyone's requests, because it would often be impossible.

Other times, it might be possible to meet a request, but not best for those concerned. For example, a father might come up to a pastor and ask that the pastor perform a wedding ceremony for his daughter, who is a Christian, and her fiance, who is not a Christian. The Bible teaches that Christians are not to marry non-Christians. So, it would violate the Bible and would not be the best for those concerned.

Another time, a request from one person might not be best for the majority. For example, the church is building a new sanctuary, and a young artist and graphics designer wants to install black lights in the ceiling and paint a mural of the Last Supper on the back wall of the sanctuary with fluorescent paint which would show up only when the black lights were on. He thinks it would make communion times special.

Well, there are all kinds of problems with that, and if you can't see them, I would not be able to explain them. The point is, you cannot, as a servant leader, meet the desires of all the people you are leading. A servant leader is not required to serve people's desires; he is required to serve people's needs. The leader must do what is best for those he is leading, as best he can determine it before God. Sometimes, this may put him in conflict with those he is leading. This was certainly true of Jesus. He came not to be served, but to serve, and yet there were many times when people objected strongly to His words and actions. Did He fail as a leader? Not at all. The people failed at following.

But when we serve others, not for self-serving reasons, but for the sake of those we are serving, then we are imitating Christ. Many people have done this well, sacrificing themselves for the sake of those they were serving. Gandhi, Abraham Lincoln, and Martin Luther King Jr. all earned a place in history because they served others for a cause higher then themselves. We are to do the same.

CONCLUSION

We are very success-oriented in the United States, and this has led to the church's putting a premium on "results." Success in the church is often measured by attendance, money, and facilities. The church with the greatest attendance, the most money, and the nicest facilities looks the most successful. Whenever a church finds a way to increase all three, that pastor is likely to be in high demand as a speaker and consultant, regardless of whether or not the church measures up to the scriptural criteria for success.

As a result, churches often put a premium on talent over godliness, ability over maturity. This has led to disastrous consequences. The Bible makes it clear that leadership in spiritual matters is not merely a matter of talent. It is a matter of spiritual gifts and spiritual maturity. If we put those two issues first and talent second, we will find a higher level of leadership being chosen for the church.

SPEED BUMP!

Slow down to be sure you have gotten the main points of this chapter.

Q1. What are the biblical positions of church leadership?

A1. The Bible mentions pastor-teachers, elders, and deacons as the *three* leadership ministries of the church.

Q2. What is the basis of leadership in the church?

A2. The basis of leadership in the church is *spiritual* maturity.

FILL IN THE BLANK

Q1. What are the biblical positions of church leadership?

A1. The Bible mentions pastor-teachers, elders, and deacons as the _____ leadership ministries of the church.

Q2. What is the basis of leadership in the church?

A2. The basis of leadership in the church is _____ maturity.

FOR FURTHER THOUGHT AND DISCUSSION

1. In the churches you know best, which leadership ministries have they had (elders, deacons, pastors)?

2. In the churches you know best, have they taken the need for spiritual maturity in their leaders seriously? What has been the result?

3. Who are the most effective leaders you have been able to observe in the church? What do you think made them effective?

WHAT IF I DON'T BELIEVE?

1. If I don't believe that leadership in the local church needs to be spiritually mature, I may suffer in my own spiritual life because of inadequate or incorrect leadership.

2. I may underestimate the impact the church can and should have in the world, because I do not have adequate models to teach and show me the possibilities.

3. I may not have a high view of the church because of inadequate respect for the leadership of my church.

FOR FURTHER STUDY

1. Scripture

- Mark 10:35–45
- Ephesians 4:11
- 1 Timothy 3:7–13

2. Books

Some other books can be helpful in studying this subject further. They are listed below in general order of difficulty. If I could read only one of these, I would read the first one.

Spiritual Leadership, J. Oswald Sanders

The Art of Leadership, Max DuPree

7

WHAT ARE THE MARKS OF SPIRITUAL MATURITY IN CHURCH LEADERS?

Much of the church is caught up in the success mania of American society. Often more concerned with budgets and building programs than with the body of Christ, the church places more emphasis on growth than on repentance. Suffering, sacrifice, and service have been preempted by success and self-fulfillment.
—**Charles Colson**

My wife and I used to live in Marietta, Georgia, a town just outside Atlanta that has been swallowed up in the suburban expansion of that dynamic city. Because it is basically as old as Atlanta, it is not just another suburb. Rather, it has a quaint character all its own. The town square is the focal point of this community where Sherman once camped during his assault on Atlanta in the Civil War. The square is the size of a city block, outlined by one-hundred-year-old (plus) trees, with grass, flowers, delightful landscaping, and an old statue or two in the center. It is a beautiful piece of history.

My office used to be just a block off the square, so I drove past it at least once a day. One day after a particularly violent thunderstorm the night before, I drove past the square to see a grand old oak tree twisted grotesquely to the ground. The wind had turned the tree around, split it open, and slammed it to the hard Georgia soil. All the other trees on the square were unharmed.

The first glance told why this tree had gone down while the others had stayed up. Unknown to anyone, the trunk of this tree had rotted out. It was hollow in the core. The only thing keeping the tree up had been the thin outer layer of wood and the bark. It had looked perfectly healthy before, just like the others. But when the test of adversity came, the tree revealed its inner rottenness by falling to the ground.

What a parable that is of spiritual leadership. For authentic spiritually mature Christian leadership, the leader must be solid to the core. If he is hollow in the middle, if there is spiritual rottenness or emptiness at the center, when the winds of temptation or adversity blow, the leader will come crashing to the ground.

Unfortunately, that is happening all too often today. From famous television preachers to obscure, unknown pastors of churches of fifty people in the middle of nowhere, spiritual leaders are crashing to the ground, their lives a heap of twisted ruins.

Warren Wiersbe, in his book *The Integrity Crisis*, has written:

> [In] the sports arena, the embassy, the halls of academe, the White House, the Pentagon, Wall Street, Capitol Hill, and even the day-care center . . . scandal seems to be the order of our day. We've had Watergate, Koreagate, and Irangate; and now . . . [in the church], Pearlygate.
>
> If [it] were only that the church is infected with hypocrites, all we would have to do is take off our masks, apologize, and start being honest again. But the matter goes much deeper. . . .We are facing an *integrity* crisis. Not only is the *conduct* of the church in question, but so is the very *character* of the church. (16–17)

Lamentably, the diagnosis is undeniable. We are in a crisis of character, and it starts at the top. Too many leaders in the church have gotten where they are, not by their spiritual maturity, but by their talents or education or political skills. But talent, education, and political skills will not keep the church healthy, safe, and forward-moving. Those things may help a minister build a personal kingdom, but not the kingdom of God.

The Bible spells out the qualifications for spiritual leaders in the church in 1 Timothy 3:1–7 and Titus 1:5–9. Specifically, Paul talks about the qualifications for elders. However, he says, immediately after discussing the qualifications for elders, that deacons likewise must be men of dignity, etc. The word "likewise" suggests that Paul does not consider deacons less mature than elders. Their spiritual maturity should be the same—only their function is different.

And, while no mention is made of the spiritual-maturity qualifications of a pastor-teacher, if an elder must be spiritually mature, it is as important or more so for a pastor to be spiritually mature. In fact, the wording of 1 Timothy 3:1–7 *(above reproach)* suggests that these marks of maturity are for everyone in the church to strive toward, not just elders. While some of the traits refer to abilities such as "able to teach," all believers are to strive to fulfill the moral qualifications. Elders must meet all the qualifications.

IN THIS CHAPTER WE LEARN THAT . . .

Twenty character qualities mentioned in the Bible mark spiritual maturity: being above reproach, the husband of one wife, temperate, prudent, respectable, hospitable, able to teach, not addicted to wine, not self-willed, not quick-tempered, not pugnacious, gentle, uncontentious, free from the love of money, one who manages his own household well, not a new convert, just, devout, self-controlled, and loving what is good.

Therefore, we can say that all three positions of leadership in the church must meet the qualifications of an elder. To encompass all three positions in a way that does not get too cumbersome verbally, I will refer to these three spiritual leadership ministries as "holding a spiritual office" in the church.

To get a picture of a spiritually mature person, we can merge the two lists in Timothy and Titus, which are very similar but not identical, and then look more closely at each of the qualifications. The actual terms used vary depending on which translation of the Bible is used. For our purposes, we will use the New American Standard Bible. Because there is overlap between the words on the two lists, and similarities of meaning among several words, we will be examining only twenty of the characteristics listed in the two passages. So that we can see where we are going, I will list the characteristics first, then look more closely at each one:

1. Above reproach
2. Husband of one wife
3. Temperate
4. Prudent
5. Respectable
6. Hospitable
7. Able to teach
8. Not addicted to wine
9. Not self-willed
10. Not quick-tempered
11. Not pugnacious
12. Gentle
13. Uncontentious
14. Free from the love of money
15. Manages his own household well
16. Not a new convert
17. Love what is good
18. Just
19. Devout
20. Self-controlled

WHAT DOES IT MEAN TO BE ABOVE REPROACH?

To be above reproach means that you have a good reputation
because you have no major character faults.

To "reproach" means "to express disapproval for a fault or offense." To be "above reproach" means that there is no fault or offense in your life for which anyone can express disapproval when it comes to moral and spiritual leadership. It does not mean you are morally perfect. No one is. We all slip or stumble from time to time. But the spiritually mature person does not have any major character flaws that destroy his reputation.

When one well-known television preacher fell into sin, I saw an interview with another equally well-known television preacher who gave the fallen preacher a tongue-lashing so severe that it took me aback. As I listened, I thought, *Well, that was a little strong, but at least I don't have to worry about that guy falling into sin.* Not long after that, it was revealed publicly that the second preacher was living in moral failure at the time he gave his public tongue-lashing to the first preacher.

He repented in tears and promised to go straight. Many people forgave him and continued to follow him. Not long after, it was revealed that he had been caught a second time in moral failure. This time, he said that his private life was nobody else's business, and showed little remorse. He is now in public disgrace.

WHY I NEED TO KNOW THIS

1. I need to know this so that I can have an accurate biblical goal to shoot for in my own life as I pursue spiritual maturity.

2. I need to be sure that I don't get involved in spiritual leadership in a church unless I am ready.

3. I need to be sure the spiritual leaders that I place myself under are also spiritually mature.

There is much that a Christian leader must know and be and do, but when you strip everything else away, a Christian leader's message is "lightness" with God. If he or she is not "right with God," he has no message. His very reason for ministry, his very foundation for ministry, his very message in ministry is destroyed. If a person is going to be a spiritual leader in the church, he must be "above reproach." There must be no major character flaw.

To be above reproach is a very broad concept, and many Bible teachers believe that it is a general category, and that all the specific traits which follow are specific examples of what it means to be above reproach. We will now look at the more specific ones.

WHAT DOES IT MEAN TO BE THE HUSBAND OF ONE WIFE?

To be the husband of one wife means, at least, that a husband is faithful to his wife in thought, word, and deed.

Not all responsible Bible teachers and scholars are agreed as to what this trait means. To translate the phrase "husband of one wife" literally, it means "a one-woman kind of man." There are several possible positions as to what this means.

1. Some believe it is prohibiting bigamy or even polygamy. Clearly, it does that.

Others believe it is not addressing this issue primarily, since having more than one wife was against the law in the Roman Empire at the time the apostle Paul wrote this letter (Gene Getz, *The Measure of a Man*, 46), and the idea would have been so inherently repugnant to Christians.

2. Some believe it is saying a man must be married to hold a spiritual office in the church.

Others believe that Paul was unmarried (1 Corinthians 7:8), and that he was an elder in the church at Ephesus while he ministered there. If so, it seems unlikely that he would have made marriage a requirement for spiritual office in the church.

3. Some believe it prohibits from spiritual office in the church a man who has remarried after his wife has died.

Others believe that, since the right to remarry after the death of a spouse is so clearly given in the Bible (Romans 7:3), this interpretation seems unlikely.

4. Some believe it prohibits a remarried divorced man from holding spiritual office in the church, because they believe remarriage after divorce is a sin (Luke 16:18).

Others believe that the Bible elsewhere appears to give permission in certain situations for divorced people to remarry (Matthew 19:9), and therefore, since good husbands are sometimes divorced by inexplicably wayward wives, the man who remarries should not be categorically eliminated from holding spiritual office in the church on this ground alone.

5. Some believe, because of the arguments against all the above positions and the wording of the phrase itself, that it is not merely addressing a man's marital status

but the issue of "moral purity." Thus it is prohibiting from spiritual office a man whose relationship with his wife or other women is not "above reproach."

6. Nearly everyone agrees that at least it means that a spiritually mature man, if he is married, should be faithful to his wife in thought, word, and deed. When looking for the marks of spiritual maturity, the character quality of "moral purity" should be true of everyone, whether single or married, man or woman. Beyond this, when looking at the qualifications for holding a spiritual office in the church, each person must be persuaded in his own mind of what else "husband of one wife" might mean.

WHAT DOES IT MEAN TO BE TEMPERATE?

To be temperate means to be self-controlled and moderate in attitude and actions.

The word the apostle Paul used here can refer to moderation in consuming alcoholic drink, but Paul deals with that issue specifically in the next verse. This term appears to be broader in meaning, referring to someone who was self-controlled and moderate in his judgment, emotions, and appetites. The King James Version translates this "be vigilant." The New International Version translates it, "keep your head in all situations." When we see how many different ways the word is used and translated, it is difficult to pin it down to one meaning.

When we combine all these ideas, we get a picture of a person who is under control because he has trained himself to use discernment. As a result, he is not given to extremes in judgment, emotions, or appetites.

Perhaps the person who exemplifies this character best in all of American history is Abraham Lincoln. His secretary of war, Edwin Stanton, had some trouble with a major general who accused him, in abusive terms, of favoritism. Stanton complained to Lincoln, who suggested that he write the officer a sharp letter of reply. Stanton did, and showed the strongly worded letter to the president, who marveled at its powerful language. "What are you going to do with that?" he asked.

Surprised at the question, Stanton said, "Send it!"

Lincoln shook his head. "You don't want to send that letter," he said. "Put it in the stove. That's what I do when I have written a letter while I am angry. It's a good letter and you had a good time writing it and feel better. Now, burn it, and write another" (*The Little, Brown Book of Anecdotes*, 360).

That is temperance in action. Lincoln was sober-minded, had good judgment, was not given to excesses in judgment, emotions, or appetites. Jesus, of course, was temperate, but sometimes it is easier to understand Jesus when we see someone who shows us by his own life what Jesus is like. If we want to be spiritually mature, we must be temperate too.

WHAT DOES IT MEAN TO BE PRUDENT?

To be prudent means to be skilled in managing practical affairs.

The original Greek word translated "prudent" can also be translated in many different ways. The word has a wide range of potential meanings, depending on the context in which it is used. It can mean "discreet," "sober," "temperate," or "sensible." The New International Version translates it "sound in mind." The *Merriam Webster Collegiate Dictionary* says that prudence is being "shrewd in the management of practical affairs." The *Oxford American Dictionary* defines it as "showing carefulness and foresight, avoiding rashness." As we compare it with the previous word, "temperate," we see that it is a close cousin.

The prudent person is extremely cautious about the consequences of his attitudes and actions, and foresighted as to what the consequences might be. That is, one person might be cautious about the consequences of his actions, but might not be particularly gifted at seeing what those consequences might be. On the other hand, a person might be foresighted as to what the consequences of attitudes and actions might be, but not very cautious about them. The prudent person is both.

WHAT DOES IT MEAN TO BE RESPECTABLE?

To be respectable means to be proper in behavior.

To be respectable requires a proper expression of behavior, not bringing disgrace or embarrassment. It has to do with the outward appearance of a person's life to others. Of course, many of the characteristics in this list are inner characteristics, so "respectability" should not be seen merely as an outward sign to others, but rather, an outward indication of the integrity that exists on the inside. Along with "temperate" and "prudent," it forms the third leg of a triad of similar characteristics that are overlapping.

There are Christians whom I believe to be sincere, who do not have good reputations, not because of a moral flaw, but because of socially embarrassing behavior. I once knew of an elderly lady who seemed to be very spiritually motivated and sincere in her Christian walk. She was, however, very unkempt. It looked as though her hair had not been washed in months. Her clothes were disorderly and profoundly out of date. She smelled of mothballs and garlic, a socially lethal combination. When she came into view, young children would freeze and gawk at her.

I would not question this lady's sincerity or walk with the Lord. Neither would I put her in a prominent position of leadership. Her behavior was not "above reproach" in the area of "respectability."

WHAT DOES IT MEAN TO BE HOSPITABLE?

To be hospitable means to be kind to strangers.

The original word for "hospitable" comes from two words that mean, literally, "love of strangers." In biblical times, there were few public houses for travelers. People were dependent on the kindness and generosity of others as they traveled. We see Joseph and Mary's predicament in Bethlehem at the time of Jesus' birth as an extreme example of the kind of thing that could happen if someone were not willing to take in the traveler.

Early Christians who were traveling evangelists and teachers were almost entirely dependent upon the willingness of other Christians to house and feed them. Otherwise the practical complications of finding a place to stay, as well as the financial burden of travel, would not allow them to continue their ministry. Therefore, the hospitable Christian gave of his time, money, and emotional energy to accommodate traveling Christians.

Paul says that an elder must be the kind of person who is willing to open his home and feed these people. At times this was not a minor inconvenience or expense.

Today, that need is not as acute as it was then, though it certainly exists on a limited basis with missionaries, evangelists, and other Christian workers. However, the habit of opening one's home for the purpose of ministry is still a significant vehicle for encouraging and ministering to others, and there still remains the need to be sensitive to strangers and others who are in need. It includes, but is not necessarily limited to, a willingness to use one's home as a tool for ministry.

WHAT DOES IT MEAN TO BE ABLE TO TEACH?

To be able to teach means that by virtue of one's life, one's knowledge, and one's ability to communicate, he is qualified to teach others.

The qualifications for being an elder deal mainly with character issues. That is, the primary qualification for being an elder is that he must *be* spiritually mature. However, an elder must also *know* things. He must be able "both to exhort in sound doctrine and to refute those who contradict" (Titus 1:9 NASB). This means he must know the Bible well enough to do this. And finally, he must *do* things. He must shepherd. He must preach and teach. He must oversee the welfare of the church. Therefore, we see three things that go together to make a person "able to teach."

First, he must meet the character requirements in the rest of the passage. Second, he must know the Bible well enough to teach and defend the truth. Third, he must be skilled enough in his communication skills to be effective in what he is trying to accomplish.

WHAT DOES IT MEAN TO NOT BE ADDICTED TO WINE?

Not addicted to wine means not drinking alcoholic beverages habitually or compulsively.

While it is not an airtight case, I think it is safe to say that most Bible teachers do not think the Bible categorically forbids drinking alcoholic beverages. The Corinthians were getting drunk on communion wine, and while Paul condemns the drunkenness, he does not condemn wine. The same is true in other passages (even here in 1 Timothy 3:3), where we would expect Paul to condemn alcohol if drinking it were categorically wrong.

However, the Bible does resoundingly condemn both drunkenness (being intoxicated, under the influence of alcohol) and addiction to alcohol (being "given to," "tarrying at," or "staying near"; using it out of habit or compulsively) (Proverbs 23:20–21, 29–35; 1 Corinthians 6:9–11; Ephesians 5:18). First Timothy 3:3 says if anyone is addicted to alcohol, he does not meet the qualification of a spiritual leader in the church.

There are significant dangers involved in drinking alcoholic beverages. No one starts out to become an alcoholic, but in drinking for personal or social reasons the individual can become trapped before he realizes it. The danger is probably greater today than in biblical times, because then they typically diluted their wine with water, significantly reducing the risk of over-drinking or getting addicted.

In addition to the personal risks, there is also the possibility of, by example, leading someone else to begin drinking who is not able to handle the alcohol, perhaps for personal or congenital reasons. Also, there is the example it sets for young people who may not have the maturity to drink alcohol responsibly. In today's cultural context, the spiritually mature person would seriously consider, before God, the wisdom of drinking alcohol. The apostle Paul wrote in Romans 14:15, 21:

For if because of food your brother is hurt, you are no longer walking according to love. Do not destroy with your food him for whom Christ died. . . . It is good not to eat meat or to drink wine, or to do anything by which your brother stumbles. (NASB)

These warnings, of course, by implication, apply to more than alcohol. Anything that is abused, is overindulged in, or has power to addict must be guarded against by the mature Christian. Certainly tobacco, drugs, and even overeating fall into the category of things that can destroy both mind and body. No one is to be ruled by anything but the Holy Spirit (1 Corinthians 6:12).

WHAT DOES IT MEAN TO NOT BE SELF-WILLED?

Not self-willed means that you do not demand your own way.

Self-will is one of the most common causes of all conflict. One person wants his way, another person wants his way, and conflict arises. The essence of not being self-willed is that a person is willing to forego his own will in matters of preference for the sake of unity and harmony.

That does not mean that just because you want something, you automatically give it up. Sometimes what a person wants is right and should be done. For example, you may want to support a building program at the church, and another person may want to start a Saturday night service to relieve Sunday morning crowding. You have a right to your position, and it is not necessary to abandon your position just because someone else wants to do something else. However, if the church should decide to start a Saturday evening service instead of building a larger sanctuary, you do not go off in a huff. If you are not self-willed, you will not insist on your position, regardless of any other consideration.

WHAT DOES IT MEAN TO NOT BE QUICK-TEMPERED?

Not quick-tempered means that you control your anger and only express anger at the things that anger God.

Anger is a major problem for many people, usually because of a blocked goal. This goes hand in hand with "not being self-willed." Personal goals get blocked all the time, and unless we have made the commitment to let God determine which of our goals are realized and which ones are not, we will have a lot of trouble with anger.

The Bible says, "But everyone must be quick to hear, slow to speak and slow to anger; for the anger of man does not achieve the righteousness of God" (James 1:19–20 NASB). And, "The discretion of a man makes him slow to anger, and his glory is to overlook a transgression" (Proverbs 19:11), and "He who is slow to anger is better than the mighty, and he who rules his spirit than he who takes [captures] a city" (Proverbs 16:32).

There are times when we cannot help but get angry. We are angry before we know what hit us. In this case, we should not sin in our anger. The apostle Paul wrote in Ephesians 4:26, "Be angry, and do not sin." Some people think that that is a command to be angry. However, the New International Version captures a better sense of the meaning: "In your anger do not sin." It could also be translated, "Though you get angry, yet do not sin." It is simply acknowledging that there are times when we cannot control whether or not we experience the emotion of anger, but we can control what we do with that emotion. Even if we do get angry, we are not to sin in our anger.

It is clear that the Bible considers anger to be a dangerous and potentially sinful emotion. The spiritually mature person will not let anger dominate him.

WHAT DOES IT MEAN NOT TO BE PUGNACIOUS?

Not to be pugnacious means that you are not a fighter, either verbally or physically.

We can hurt people grievously with our words, and we can injure them seriously with violence. Neither characteristic is true of the spiritually mature person. The word *pugnacious* literally means "a striker," so it has the central meaning of "violence." The spiritually mature person does not resort to verbal or physical violence.

WHAT DOES IT MEAN TO BE GENTLE?

To be gentle means to treat with care, so as to soothe and not to hurt.

The basic word for "gentle" in the Bible means to be "fitting, equitable," and therefore to be fair, moderate, patient, expressing considerateness. It means that you do not run roughshod over other people. Rather you treat them with respect. Gentleness is often interpreted merely as a lack of roughness. Such is not the case, however. Gentleness is not only all absence of roughness but the presence of fairness, respect, and carefulness. Many church conflicts occur because the leaders are not gentle. A spirit of gentleness would head off many conflicts in congregational meetings, board meetings, and other situations. If someone is not gentle, he does not qualify for spiritual leadership.

WHAT DOES IT MEAN TO BE UNCONTENTIOUS?

To be uncontentious means that you are not quarrelsome or argumentative.

Many of the qualities of spiritual maturity overlap, and certainly a person would not be gentle and contentious at the same time. However, the apostle Paul wanted to be specific on the types of characteristics that mark a spiritually mature person. We have all known persons who have a hair-trigger when it comes to arguing or quarreling with others. Some people love to argue; most do not, however, and find it terribly uncomfortable to deal with someone who does. Being quarrelsome or argumentative disqualifies one from holding leadership in the church.

WHAT DOES IT MEAN TO BE FREE FROM THE LOVE OF MONEY?

To be free from the love of money means that you do not want money more than you want the will of God.

Many people think the Bible says that money is the root of all evil. It does not. It says that "the love of money is a root of all kinds of evil" (1 Timothy 6:10), and "some have strayed from the faith in their greediness, and pierced themselves through with many sorrows." There is nothing wrong with money. It is a resource, like good health and intelligence. Money is neither good nor bad. The thing that is good or bad is our attitude toward it.

There are a number of ways that a love of money manifests itself. Someone might spend money like crazy, or someone might be exceptionally stingy, miserly. Both can reflect a love of money, with opposite responses.

Someone who is willing to put the will of God above the desire for money will give faithfully to the ministry, be as generous to the disadvantaged as his circumstances allow, and see money as a tool to advance the kingdom of God. It does not mean that one cannot make a lot of money. Many people who are free from the love of money are very wealthy.

LeTourneau, an industrial inventor, was extremely wealthy. As a Christian, he asked the Lord how he should use his money, and decided that instead of tithing 10 percent and living on 90, he would tithe 90 percent and live on 10 percent. Even then, he lived very comfortably, but it showed his spirit toward money. He wanted the will of God more than money.

Christians are not probited from desiring to make money. I wish more Christian entrepreneurs would make more money, so that they would have more to give away. Often, ministry is limited only by the amount of money that is given to it.

I have a friend who stands on the threshold of a simple, small business that has breathtaking financial potential. He asked me what I thought he should do. He was willing not to embark on the enterprise if I thought it would be wrong for him to make that much money. My advice to him was what John Wesley once said: "Make all you can, save all you can, give all you can."

Money is all right. Just don't love it. Don't be in bondage to it. Don't let it keep you from following the will of God. Don't let the love of it keep you from helping others when it is in your power to do so. Don't let it keep you from being generous in the support of ministries.

WHAT DOES IT MEAN TO MANAGE ONE'S HOUSEHOLD WELL?

To manage one's household well means to lead one's family with care and diligence.

The Greek word here for "manage" means "to stand before," that is, "to lead, attend to." It carries with it the idea of care and diligence.

The Bible instructs fathers that they are not to exasperate or provoke their children to anger but are to nurture their children in the admonition of the Lord, to discipline their children using biblical principles, to love their family with a sacrificial love, and to lead their family members in the way in which they should go (Proverbs 22:6; Ephesians 6:4).

Today many Christian fathers are passive, having little or no involvement in the guidance and development of the lives of their children. Of those who are involved, many Christians are more influenced by the philosophies of the world in rearing their children than they are by the Bible. As a result, many well-meaning Christians have undisciplined children who are often an embarrassment to them and who frequently rebel in teenage years. The subject is a huge one, and not one that can be dealt with in depth in a chapter like this. But parents must not let cultural values replace biblical instruction when it comes to rearing children. (Perhaps James Dobson has addressed this subject in his many books as well as any one author today, and it would be valuable for any parent to become familiar with his writings.)

WHAT DOES IT MEAN NOT TO BE A NEW CONVERT?

Not to be a new convert means that sufficient time has passed since becoming a Christian.

It is easy to understand what "not a new convert" means. Literally, it means "newly planted," and in this context, means that a person is not a new Christian. However, it is less certain how much time must pass before a person is no longer a new convert.

When the apostle Paul and Timothy and Titus were establishing new churches, no one had been a convert for more than a few years. So "not a new convert" does not mean that a person must have been a Christian for twenty-five years. But on the other hand, he must have been a Christian long enough to validate that he is a firmly committed Christian, has experienced the life-change necessary to reflect these character qualities, and has learned the Bible well enough to teach it and to guard the church against false teaching.

Not only must these practical matters be taken into consideration, but the apostle Paul also mentions another: that, as a new Christian, he is in danger of becoming conceited (1 Timothy 3:6). Apparently there is a danger of pride if a new convert assumes a position of spiritual leadership too soon. Because different people mature at different rates, and some have farther to go than others when they become Christians, no length of time can be fixed for all people. But the Christian must not be a new convert, and the church must use these principles and the Lord's leading to decide a specific case.

WHAT DOES IT MEAN TO LOVE WHAT IS GOOD?

To love what is good means that we choose to do good rather than evil.

The world seems torn between good and evil. When you look at the Red Cross, the Salvation Army, Goodwill Industries, all the hospitals, all the schools, all the social relief agencies, all the social help agencies, the amount of good that is done in the world is amazing.

At the same time, when you read in the newspapers about the terrorism, the wars, the victimization of the helpless, the crime, and the sexual sin, the evil in the world is equally amazing. The world seems divided in half.

That should not surprise us too much, because the line between good and evil does not run only through countries and cities and world views, but also through every human heart. Each of us is capable of doing good or evil. The spiritually mature person is one who, while not perfect, has established a track record for choosing good over evil.

WHAT DOES IT MEAN TO BE JUST?

To be just means to give equal weight to all people and actions.

Many unjust things go on in our world. People who are guilty go free, and people who are innocent are convicted. A wealthy businessman in a liberal city can pay enough slick lawyers to get him acquitted of multimillion-dollar fraud, while a poor man in a conservative city gets the book thrown at him. But one day, we will all stand before the Great Judge, and we will be evaluated according to standards applied equally to all people. Final and true justice will be served. The spiritually mature person must try to envision, with a mind instructed by the Scriptures and a heart sensitized through prayer, what God would do in any given situation, and try to be just in all things.

WHAT DOES IT MEAN TO BE DEVOUT?

To be devout means to earnestly pursue one's faith.

Plenty of people are religious. They go to church each Sunday, tithe their money, and say grace before meals. Unless a person does this from the heart, however, he is not devout. On the other hand, a person may claim to be devout but never go to church, pray, or give money to the cause of Christ; this person is not devout either. Being devout means earnestly pursuing all the things a Christian should do, but with a right heart.

WHAT DOES IT MEAN TO BE SELF-CONTROLLED?

To be self-controlled means to be personally disciplined in all things.

To be self-controlled means that you have gained enough mastery over your attitudes and actions that you are able to get yourself to do the things you should do and keep yourself from doing the things you shouldn't. We have all made New Year's resolutions, only to have them die of neglect. We have all turned over a new leaf, only to have the leaf roll back over when we weren't looking. No one does absolutely everything he ought to do all the time.

However, self-control is, in large measure, the difference between success and failure in life. Nearly everyone can get a pretty good vision of what he could and should do. But what separates the mature from the immature is whether or not he follows through on what he could and should do.

If a person does not have a track record of being self-controlled, he is missing a mark of spiritual maturity and does not qualify for leadership in the church.

CONCLUSION

We have taken a number of pages just to say one thing: spiritual leaders in the church must be spiritually mature. Water seeks its own level. A congregation will rise no higher, as a whole, than its leadership. If the leadership is shallow and hypocritical, most people will not be willing to stay there; they will move on. The only people who will stay under that kind of leadership are people who are willing to put up with shallowness and hypocrisy.

Paul has done the church a great favor by spelling out in detail what a spiritual leader must be like. Those of us who lead must measure ourselves by that standard, and be willing to step aside, even if temporarily, until our lives are a basic (not perfect)reflection of these character qualities. Those of us who follow must require that our leaders manifest these qualities. If they do not, we must put ourselves under the spiritual leadership of those who do.

SPEED BUMP!

Slow down to be sure you have gotten the main points of this chapter.

Q1. What does it mean to be above reproach?

A1. To be above reproach means that you have a *good reputation* because you have no major character faults.

Q2. What does it mean to be the husband of one wife?

A2. To be the husband of one wife means, at least, that a husband is *faithful* to his wife in thought, word, and deed.

Q3. What does it mean to be temperate?

A3. To be temperate means to be self-controlled and *moderate* in attitude and actions.

Q4. What does it mean to be prudent?

A4. To be prudent means to be *skilled* in managing practical affairs.

Q5. What does it mean to be respectable?

A5. To be respectable means to be *proper* in behavior.

Q6. What does it mean to be hospitable?

A6. To be hospitable means to be *kind* to strangers.

Q7. What does it mean to be able to teach?

A7. To be able to teach means that by virtue of one's life, one's knowledge, and one's ability to communicate, he is *qualified* to teach others.

Q8. What does it mean to not be addicted to wine?

A8. Not addicted to wine means not drinking alcoholic beverages habitually or *compulsively.*

Q9. What does it mean to not be self-willed?

A9. Not self-willed means that you do not *demand* your own way.

Q10. What does it mean to not be quick-tempered?

A10. Not quick-tempered means that you *control* your anger and only express anger at the things that anger God.

Q11. What does it mean not to be pugnacious?

A11. Not to be pugnacious means that you are not *a fighter,* either verbally or physically.

Q12. What does it mean to be gentle?

A12. To be gentle means to treat with *care,* so as to soothe and not to hurt.

Q13. What does it mean to be uncontentious?

A13. To be uncontentious means that you are not quarrelsome or *argumentative.*

Q14. What does it mean to be free from the love of money?

A14. To be free from the love of money means that you do not *want* money more than you want the will of God.

Q15. What does it mean to manage one's household well?

A15. To manage one's household well means to *lead* one's family with care and diligence.

Q16. What does it mean not to be a new convert?

A16. Not to be a new convert means that sufficient *time* has passed since becoming a Christian.

Q17. What does it mean to love what is good?

A17. To love what is good means that we *choose* to do good rather than evil.

Q18. What does it mean to be just?

A18. To be just means to give *equal* weight to all people and actions.

Q19. What does it mean to be devout?

A19. To be devout means to earnestly *pursue* one's faith.

Q20. What does it mean to be self-controlled?

A20. To be self-controlled means to be personally *disciplined* in all things.

FILL IN THE BLANK

Q1. What does it mean to be above reproach?

A1. To be above reproach means that you have a _____ _____ because you have no major character faults.

Q2. What does it mean to be the husband of one wife?

A2. To be the husband of one wife means, at least, that a husband is _____ to his wife in thought, word, and deed.

Q3. What does it mean to be temperate?

A3. To be temperate means to be self-controlled and _____ in attitude and actions.

Q4. What does it mean to be prudent?

A4. To be prudent means to be _____ in managing practical affairs.

Q5. What does it mean to be respectable?

A5. To be respectable means to be _____ in behavior.

Q6. What does it mean to be hospitable?

A6. To be hospitable means to be _____ to strangers.

Q7. What does it mean to be able to teach?

A7. To be able to teach means that by virtue of one's life, one's knowledge, and one's ability to communicate, he is _____ to teach others.

Q8. What does it mean to not be addicted to wine?

A8. Not addicted to wine means not drinking alcoholic beverages habitually or _____ .

Q9. What does it mean to not be self-willed?

A9. Not self-willed means that you do not _____ your own way.

Q10. What does it mean to not be quick-tempered?

A10. Not quick-tempered means that you _____ your anger and only express anger at the things that anger God.

Q11. What does it mean not to be pugnacious?

A11. Not to be pugnacious means that you are not a _____ , either verbally or physically.

Q12. What does it mean to be gentle?

A12. To be gentle means to treat with _____ , so as to soothe and not to hurt.

Q13. What does it mean to be uncontentious?

A13. To be uncontentious means that you are not quarrelsome or _____ .

Q14. What does it mean to be free from the love of money?

A14. To be free from the love of money means that you do not _____ money more than you want the will of God.

Q15. What does it mean to manage one's household well?

A15. To manage one's household well means to _____ one's family with care and diligence.

Q16. What does it mean not to be a new convert?

A16. Not to be a new convert means that sufficient _____ has passed since becoming a Christian.

Q17. What does it mean to love what is good?

A17. To love what is good means that we _____ to do good rather than evil.

Q18. What does it mean to be just?

A18. To be just means to give _____ weight to all people and actions.

Q19. What does it mean to be devout?

A19. To be devout means to earnestly _____ one's faith.

Q20. What does it mean to be self-controlled?

A20. To be self-controlled means to be personally _____ in all things.

FOR FURTHER THOUGHT AND DISCUSSION

1. Which qualities of an elder do you think you are strongest in? Do you know why you are strong in those areas?

2. What qualities do you think you are weakest in? Do you know why you are weak in those areas?

3. What do you think you could/should do to capitalize on your strengths and overcome your weaknesses? Is there any insight from your strong areas that you can use to build up your weak areas?

WHAT IF I DON'T BELIEVE?

1. If I don't believe that these qualities are the marks of a spiritually mature person, I may contribute to weakening the character of the church by overlooking the need for spiritual maturity in the leaders of the church I attend.

2. I may not take them seriously enough in my own life. I may be content to tolerate significant weaknesses in some areas, rationalizing that "no one is perfect."

3. I may fall into the trap of trying to function as a spiritual leader in a church even though I don't meet the qualifications.

FOR FURTHER STUDY

1. Scripture

- 1 Timothy 3:1–7
- Titus 1:5–9

2. Book

The Measure of a Man, Gene Getz

8

WHAT ARE THE ORDINANCES OF THE CHURCH?

The world drinks to forget. The Christian drinks to remember.
—Steve Brown

I t is a proverb in America that a picture is worth a thousand words. We draw pictures or diagrams on a paper napkin at lunch, for example, because it is easier than explaining only in words what we have to communicate. In addition to real pictures, we use word pictures or analogies. We say, for example, that trying to solve a difficult problem is like hitting your head against a brick wall.

If we use both real and word pictures to communicate, it should come as no surprise to us that God uses pictures and word pictures. He has pictured death and resurrection by giving us the seasons in a year. Summer is life. Winter is death. Spring is resurrection. He also uses word pictures. In Mark 4:30, Jesus asks the question, "How shall we picture the kingdom of God?" Then He answers by saying, "It is like a mustard seed, which, when sown upon the soil, though it is smaller than all the seeds that are upon the soil, yet when it is sown, it grows up and becomes larger than all the garden plants and forms large branches; so that the birds of the air can nest under its shade" (vv. 31–32 NASB).

In addition, God has given us many symbolic pictures. For example, the architecture and layout of the tabernacle and the temple in the Old Testament were designed to picture sin, death, separation from God, forgiveness, and new life. All that in the Old Testament was a picture of the fact that Jesus was to come and be our final sacrifice, making the animal sacrifices unnecessary.

In the New Testament, Jesus gave us two symbolic pictures of eternal truths He wants us to observe until He returns, in order to make sure that those truths

113

are never lost. Those two pictures are baptism and the Lord's Supper, or communion. The Lord's Supper is a picture of Jesus' death and resurrection, and baptism is a picture of our death and resurrection. These are two critical truths in the New Testament, which is why Jesus intends for the church to "picture" these two truths until He returns.

IN THIS CHAPTER WE LEARN THAT . . .

1. Baptism is a symbolic act in which Christians proclaim their belief in Jesus' death and resurrection.

2. There are three views as to what happens when we are baptized: the Catholic view, the Covenant view, and the Baptist view.

3. While there are responsible differences of perspective, everyone believes that all adult believers should be baptized, and some believe that all children of Christians should be baptized.

4. There are three forms of baptism: sprinkling, pouring, and immersion.

5. The Lord's Supper is a ceremonial meal of bread and the fruit of the vine commemorating the death of Jesus for our sins, and celebrating His new covenant with us.

We call baptism and the Lord's Supper "ordinances" because they were "ordained" or established and required by Jesus. Baptism is a "once-for-all" rite, while the Lord's Supper is to be an ongoing and regular rite of remembrance.

WHAT IS BAPTISM?

Baptism is a symbolic act in which Christians proclaim their belief in Jesus' death and resurrection.

The physical act of baptism is the sprinkling, pouring, or immersing (complete submerging) of a person in water. It is a simple gesture, yet once we understand it, it has deep and profound meaning. God intended it to be a sign of inward cleansing of sin (Acts 22:16), and a sign of receiving spiritual life (Titus 3:5).

Immersion in water symbolizes death (being buried in the water) and resurrection (coming back up out of the water). It is symbolic of our union with Christ

114

WHAT ARE THE ORDINANCES OF THE CHURCH?

(much as the union of a husband and wife in marriage, where the two become one) in His death, burial, and resurrection (Romans 6:3–7; Colossians 2:11–12).

The imagery of sprinkling or pouring water on a person is not quite so graphic, yet it symbolizes the cleansing of sin as the water washes over us.

WHAT HAPPENS WHEN WE ARE BAPTIZED?

*There are three views as to what happens when we are baptized: the
Catholic view, the Covenant view, and the Baptist view.*

The Christian world is not united in its understanding of what happens when we are baptized. While all three traditions base their views on Scripture, they also go beyond the Scripture, "filling in the blanks" as it were, in places where the Bible is not explicit in its instruction. Therefore, while all three claim biblical support for their positions, there is also room for responsible differences of opinion.

The Catholic View

Roman Catholics believe that the Roman Catholic Church was established by Jesus to bring the grace of God to each person. When a priest baptizes a person, that person receives new life in Christ. As each person received the guilt of original sin from Adam, so each person can receive forgiveness and new life in Christ through baptism. By baptism, the child or convert is not fully saved but is "born again" to begin his or her lifelong quest of full salvation (Bruce Shelley, *Why Baptism?*, 20). Since this grace is so important, everyone should be baptized. Infants are baptized for obvious reasons, and converted adults must also be. While baptism is sufficient for salvation if not obstructed, adults can obstruct, through sin and/or unbelief, the saving grace of God brought by baptism. That is, if they simply don't believe in Christ or knowingly turn their backs on the truth, the grace can be obstructed by those who have been baptized, according to the Catholic view.

The Covenant View

Most Protestant churches other than those in the Baptist tradition, including many independent churches, hold to the Covenant view of baptism. This includes most Presbyterians, Episcopalians, Methodists, and Lutherans. The explanation of the Covenant view varies somewhat from teacher to teacher, and so there may be those who hold to the Covenant view who will not think that I have represented their view adequately. However, in the reading and research I have done, I believe the following explanation will represent accurately a reputable and widely held position.

## WHY I NEED TO KNOW THIS

1. I need to understand what baptism and the Lord's Supper mean to God, so that I can understand them fully and try to invest them with as much meaning as God does.

2. I need to understand that baptism and the Lord's Supper are viewed differently by different denominations and churches, and if I have deep convictions about them, I may need to choose a church that has the same convictions as I do.

3. I need to understand that godly and knowledgeable people differ in their understanding as to the meaning and mode of baptism and the Lord's Supper, and that whatever I believe, I must respect other responsible views on the matters.

The Continuing Covenant. Baptism is viewed as a sign of the new covenant in Christ. A covenant is an agreement or contract between two parties. Marriage is a covenant between a man and a woman to remain faithful to the partner until death. The sign of the marriage covenant in our culture is a ring on the third finger of the left hand.

God has made a number of covenants with humanity, and each one has had a sign. After the Flood, for example, God made a covenant with Noah that He would never again destroy the world through a flood. The sign of that agreement was the rainbow (Genesis 11:8–17). When we see a rainbow today, we are assured of God's agreement never again to flood the earth.

God made a covenant with Abraham to offer salvation to him and his descendants in return for their faith. God promised to give Abraham land, descendants, and eternal blessing. In return, He asked for Abraham's faith, which he was to demonstrate by being obedient to God. The sign of this covenant was circumcision. "You shall be circumcised in the flesh of your foreskin, and it shall be the sign of the covenant between Me and you" (Genesis 17:11 NASB).

This covenant sign lasts throughout the Old Testament. In the New Testament, however, a new covenant is established by Jesus (1 Corinthians 11:23–26). The old covenant is replaced with a new covenant, an agreement by God to give humanity salvation by grace through faith in Jesus.

> Our covenant-making God approaches Abraham in sheer grace. Abraham responds in faith: "And he [Abraham] believed the Lord; and he reckoned it to him as righteousness" (Genesis 15:6). The grace of God is met by the faith of Abraham. That is how Abraham was put right with God. That is how you are. There is no other way. There never has been. Do not believe those who tell you that there was one way of

salvation in the Old Testament (law keeping), but that God has now changed his mind and decided that faith would be a better idea! Men and women were saved in the Old Testament in just the same way as they were in the New Testament—by the sheer undeserved generosity of God, to which they respond in adoring trust: the grace-faith reciprocal. That is how it has always been with God, and always will be. God's grace: all of him for us. Our faith: all of us for him. (Michael Green, *Baptism*, 24)

Baptism is the sign of the new covenant of Jesus. We are no longer to be circumcised, but we are now to be baptized.

Result of Baptism. Baptism does not, in this view, result in the person's automatically receiving new life in Christ, as in the Catholic view (James Packer, *Concise Theology*, 213). "Baptism is a sign of the promise of God of salvation to all who believe in Christ" (R. C. Sproul, *Essential Truths of the Christian Faith*, 225). "Therefore, it is primarily a testimony to God's promises in the gospel rather than a testimony to our faith" (Green, 77). Baptism is a testimony to God's declaration of His acceptance and justification of sinners who receive His Son.

When we are baptized, we testify to the fact that it is God who has offered this covenant of grace to us, and that, if we follow His way, we will enter fully into His salvation. Therefore, just as infants were circumcised in the old covenant, infants may be baptized in the new covenant, since the act is a testimony to God's work and not our volitional act.

The Baptist View

Not all who hold to a "Baptist" view of baptism are Baptists by denomination. This view is held by nearly all who do not hold to a Catholic or Covenant view, and includes many denominations and independent traditions.

The Baptist view understands that baptism is a sign, a picture, a memorial of our redemption in Christ. It is a visual sermon of a central truth, that as Jesus died and was raised again to new life, so, when we received Him as our personal Savior, we were crucified with Him and raised to new life (Galatians 2:20). This is described as "believer's baptism" and is a sign of our having received Christ as our personal Savior.

WHO IS BAPTIZED?

While there are responsible differences of perspective, everyone believes that all adult converts should be baptized, and some believe that all children of Christians should be baptized.

The Catholic View

The Roman Catholic view is that, since spiritual rebirth is imparted through baptism, including the baptism of infants, all people should be baptized.

The Covenant View

Those who hold the Covenant view do not believe that spiritual rebirth is accomplished merely through baptism. However, some who hold this view come very close to this position, stating that baptism "is normally seen as effecting what it proclaims, the new birth of the candidate" (Green, 64), though "it is not ... invariably or unconditionally efficacious, as some ... would suggest" (63).

The case for baptizing infants is neither commanded nor forbidden in the New Testament. Its practice is based on the understanding that the old covenant with Abraham and the new covenant in Christ are in principle the same. Abraham came to faith as an adult and was circumcised as an adult as a sign of the covenant God had made with him. His son, Isaac, on the other hand, received the sign of circumcision as an infant, by the command of God. Again, it was as a sign of the covenant God had made with Abraham and his descendants.

Being circumcised did not mean that Isaac had come to faith in God. That was clearly impossible because of his age. Rather, it was a sign, to be perpetuated through the generations, that God had made a covenant with Abraham and all his descendants.

Baptism. In this way, the covenant understanding of baptism is much closer to the role of the Lord's Supper. We perpetuate the Lord's Supper through the generations to give testimony to the salvation that is available to us through the death and resurrection of Christ. We do not experience that salvation unless, in an understanding way, we consciously receive it. In the same way, we perpetuate baptism through the generations to give testimony to the agreement that God has made to us that if we will receive Christ by faith, we will receive the gift of eternal life.

In the Old Testament, adult converts and infants of Jewish families were circumcised. Therefore, in the New Testament, adult converts and infants of Christian families are to be baptized.

Confirmation. It is recognized by most who hold the Covenant view that infant baptism does not automatically result in the eternal salvation of the one baptized. Therefore, those who are baptized as infants should be discipled, instructed, and nurtured in the Christian faith until such a time as they come to personal faith in Christ. When this happens, it is valuable for the person to personally affirm the truth that was spoken over him when he was baptized. This is done in a number of denominations in a ceremony called "confirmation." It is an opportunity for the person to confirm personally the truth that baptism represented.

This practice of confirmation is not found in Scripture. However, it is interesting that "the Jew, circumcised on the eighth day, had to take upon himself 'the yoke of the Law' in the bar *mitzvah* ceremony at about the age of twelve, so those baptized in infancy need to have an opportunity to take their personal stand for Christ, and make their own what has been confidently hoped and prayed for on their behalf at their baptism. Confirmation provides just this" (Green, 102).

The Baptist View

The Baptist view is that all the clear passages in the New Testament telling of baptisms are the result of belief in Christ. Therefore, the Baptists see baptism as public profession of the believer's faith, the official sign that they are, in fact, identifying with Christ. Baptism is the final step of obedience in professing their faith in Christ.

Believers who are confessing faith in Christ for the first time, who happen to have been baptized as infants, are often rebaptized, since Baptists recognize "believer's baptism" and the infant was not a believer. Who is baptized, then, in the Baptist tradition? Only those who have knowledgeably confessed faith in Christ.

HOW ARE WE TO BAPTIZE?

There are three forms of baptism: sprinkling, pouring, and immersion.

The Bible does not explicitly state how we are to baptize. The word in Greek, the original language of the New Testament, is *baptizo*, which means primarily "to dunk or immerse," although pouring or sprinkling are entirely possible meanings of the word. As a symbolic picture of our union with the death and resurrection of Christ, immersion is certainly the most graphic form of baptism. Also, in an account when John the Baptist was preaching and baptizing, the Bible makes a point of saying that he did so in a location where there was much water. This suggests (but does not prove) that he was immersing (John 3:23). Also, when John baptized Jesus, they were standing in the water, another possible indication of immersion. On the other hand, in another account in which thousands came to Christ and were baptized in a very short period of time in a location where there was not an abundance of water, the implication is that, because of the lack of time and water, they might have sprinkled or poured. Either would have required significantly less time and water than immersion (Acts 2:41).

Sprinkling or pouring are the methods of choice in infant baptism. Some churches give adult converts their choice of method for baptism.

Even among those who immerse, there is not absolute agreement. Most Baptists baptize once backward in the name of the Father, Son, and Holy Spirit. Some Brethren, on the other hand, baptize three times forward, once in the name of the Father, once in the name of the Son, and once in the name of the Holy Spirit, fulfilling the command in Matthew 28:19–20 to baptize in the name (not names) of the Father and of the Son and of the Holy Spirit.

All are agreed, however, that baptism is a step of obedience to Christ and that baptism is a picture of our union with Christ in His death and resurrection.

WHAT IS THE LORD'S SUPPER?

The Lord's Supper is a ceremonial meal of bread and the fruit of the vine commemorating the death of Jesus for our sins, and celebrating His new covenant with us.

The central passage of Scripture dealing with the Lord's Supper is 1 Corinthians 11:23–26:

> For I received from the Lord that which I also delivered to you: that the Lord Jesus on the same night in which He was betrayed took bread; and when He had given thanks, He broke it and said, "Take, eat; this is My body which is broken for you; do this in remembrance of Me." In the same manner He also took the cup after supper, saying, "This cup is the new covenant in My blood. This do, as often as you drink it, in remembrance of Me." For as often as you eat this bread and drink this cup, you proclaim the Lord's death till He comes.

This passage tells us the following:

1. Jesus instituted the Lord's Supper.

2. It is to be observed in the church until He returns to earth.

3. It is to be a perpetual remembrance of His sacrifice.

4. It symbolizes the new covenant that He established with us, to grant us forgiveness of sin and eternal salvation by grace through faith in Jesus Christ.

Considerable controversy has existed through the centuries over the nature of the elements (the bread and wine). Three views predominate today.

Transubstantiation

Trans means "to go beyond." *Transubstantiation* means "to go beyond the substance." Roman Catholics believe that the substance of the bread and wine are miraculously transformed, actually *becoming* the body and blood of Jesus, even though they still appear to be bread and wine. Jesus said, "This is My body which is broken for you" and, "This cup is the new covenant in My blood" (1 Corinthians 11:24–25). The Roman Catholics take those words literally. "Transubstantiation" is their explanation for how the words can be literally true, and yet the elements appear to the human eye to be unchanged.

Consubstantiation

Con means "with." Lutherans believe that Christ's body and blood come to be present *in*, *with*, and under the substance of the bread and wine, which become, as a result, more than bread and wine, but not less, resulting in *consubstantiation*. The Eastern Orthodox churches and some Anglican churches believe the same.

Representation

Most other Protestants believe either that the elements are only a symbolic or ceremonial meal, or that by faith the believer, during communion, enters into a special spiritual union with the risen Christ. They believe that the phrase "this is My body . . . My blood" means that the bread and wine *represent* His body and blood, not that they actually *become* His body and blood, or that His body and blood come *with* the bread and wine. Jesus frequently used such figures of speech. He said, "I am the door," and "I am the true vine," yet we do not insist that He be made of wood or leaves.

All Protestants believe that at the Lord's Supper we are giving thanks to Christ for His finished and accepted work of atonement, rather than mystically repeating His crucifixion, as the Roman Catholics believe.

The prescribed ritual of the Supper has three levels of meaning for participants. First, it has a past reference to Christ's death that we remember. Second, it has a present reference to our corporate feeding on Him by faith, with implications for how we treat our fellow believers (1 Corinthians 11:20–22). Third, it has a future reference as we look ahead to Christ's return and are encouraged by the thought of it.

WHAT YOU NEED TO KNOW ABOUT THE CHURCH

Preliminary self-exam, to make sure one's frame of mind is as it should be, is advised (1 Corinthians 11:28), and the wisdom of the advice is obvious (Packer, 219).

CONCLUSION

These two ordinances, baptism and the Lord's Supper, are the two divinely ordained activities that all the church is to participate in—baptism once, and the Lord's Supper perpetually. The renowned Westminster Confession states that the effect of participating in the ordinances is "to put a visible difference between those that belong unto the church and the rest of the world, and solemnly to engage them to the service of God in Christ, according to his word" (XXVII.l).

Some believe that in observing the ordinances, divine grace is given to us. Others contend that there is no grace given through the ordinances, that they are purely symbolic and ceremonial rites.

Perhaps there is a middle ground that many may find attractive. Could we not see the ordinances as a means of grace in the sense that God uses them to strengthen our faith and to encourage acts of faith in response to the privilege of being part of God's covenant? If the ordinances produce grace in us, it is not because of the minister, but because God chooses to increase our faith and service to Him. As the preaching of the Word makes the gospel audible, so the ordinances make it visible, and God can increase our faith both by preaching and by the ordinances. The ordinances can impart grace in the sense that *seeing* can increase our *believing*.

SPEED BUMP!

Slow down to be sure you have gotten the main points of this chapter.

Q1. What is baptism?

A1. Baptism is a symbolic act in which Christians *proclaim* their belief in Jesus' death and resurrection.

Q2. What happens when we are baptized?

A2. There are *three* views as to what happens when we are baptized: the Catholic view, the Covenant view, and the Baptist view.

Q3. Who is baptized?

A3. While there are responsible *differences* of perspective, everyone believes that all adult believers should be baptized, and some believe that all children of Christians should be baptized.

Q4. How are we to baptize?

A4. There are *three* forms of baptism: sprinkling, pouring, and immersion.

Q5. What is the Lord's Supper?

A5. The Lord's Supper is a ceremonial meal of bread and the fruit of the vine *commemorating* the death of Jesus for our sins, and celebrating His new covenant with us.

FILL IN THE BLANK

Q1. What is baptism?

A1. Baptism is a symbolic act in which Christians _____ their belief in Jesus' death and resurrection.

Q2. What happens when we are baptized?

A2. There are _____ views as to what happens when we are baptized: the Catholic view, the Covenant view, and the Baptist view.

Q3. Who is baptized?

A3. While there are responsible _____ of perspective, everyone believes that all adult believers should be baptized, and some believe that all children of Christians should be baptized.

Q4. How are we to baptize?

A4. There are _____ forms of baptism: sprinkling, pouring, and immersion.

Q5. What is the Lord's Supper?

A5. The Lord's Supper is a ceremonial meal of bread and the fruit of the vine _____ the death of Jesus for our sins, and celebrating His new covenant with us.

FOR FURTHER THOUGHT AND DISCUSSION

1. If you have church experience, what has been the perspective on baptism that you are most familiar with?

2. What do you think are the strengths and weaknesses of your position? What do you think are the strengths and weaknesses of the other positions?

3. What is the perspective on the elements of the Lord's Supper that you are most familiar with?

4. What do you think are the strengths and weaknesses of your position? What do you think are the strengths and weaknesses of the other positions?

WHAT IF I DON'T BELIEVE?

1. If I don't believe in the biblical teachings of the importance of the ordinances, I fail to appreciate the profound sacrifice that Jesus made, which the ordinances commemorate. I don't see them as important as God does.

2. I miss out on the depth of worship that is available to Christians when they enter into the ordinances with an awareness of their significance.

3. I fail to convey to others the lessons that the ordinances are intended to picture.

FOR FURTHER STUDY

1. Scripture

- Matthew 3:13–17
- Matthew 28:19–20
- 1 Corinthians 11:23–34

2. Books

Other books can be helpful in studying this subject further. If I could read only one of these, I would read the first one.

Baptism, Michael Green (Covenant View)

The Church: God's People, Bruce Shelley (Baptist View)

9

HOW SHOULD THE CHURCH BE GOVERNED?

All life on earth seems to require some sort of form. It is tough to think of formless life. Even a jellyfish has a basic shape. Certainly, in human affairs spirit must express itself in visible structures before it can make a contribution to the ongoing drama of history.

—Bruce Shelley

When I was a boy, I used to play with gunpowder. It was foolish, I know, but I did it anyway. My two older brothers taught me how. It was their fault! Don't ask me where I got the gunpowder. You don't want to know.

I would pile half a cup of gunpowder in one lump, then dribble a little path of gunpowder for a couple of feet leading away from the pile, to act as a fuse. Then I would light the fuse and back up fast. The fuse would fizzle and hiss as it stormed furiously toward the pile of gunpowder. There would be a big "FFFOOOOOFFFF!!" A small mushroom cloud would rise ominously into the air as I watched in undisguised awe.

I learned that if you controlled the fire just a bit, you could get some direction out of it. A boyhood friend of mine showed me how to take a small handful of wooden matches with all the match heads together and wrap aluminum foil tightly around just the heads. Then he struck a match and touched the flame to the aluminum foil. When it got hot enough, all the matches inside the foil lit, and the whole thing took off like a primitive moon rocket. The first time we tried it was on his enclosed back porch (without the supervision of his parents, I'm afraid) and we nearly set the house on fire. It bounced, sputtering and smoking, off all the walls and ceiling before "running out of fuel."

My next experiment was with firecrackers (which, of course, are filled with gunpowder)—not the little pop-pop-pop kind, but the big "KA-BOOM!" kind, called cherry bombs and M-80s. Again, my older brothers and cousins showed me how to do this. I was totally innocent! But we got a Donald Duck orange juice can, a Campbell's soup can, a Van Camp's pork and beans can, and a big Hawaiian Punch can. Then, (and timing was everything!) we lit a cherry bomb, put it in the orange juice can, put that upside down in the soup can, put that upside down in the pork and beans can, and put that upside down in the Hawaiian Punch can, then *ran like crazy*!! The cans blew sky-high. (You may want to keep this book out of the hands of your children until they are old enough to know better.)

My final and most responsible experiences with gunpowder had to do with firearms. My family (grandparents, uncles, cousins) all had firearms, and I learned to shoot at a fairly early age. I will never forget firing our vintage twelve-gauge shotgun for the first time. I was about eleven or twelve, and it nearly knocked me to the ground. But I became a fairly accurate marksman with a twenty-two gauge rifle and was a safe and responsible gunman (except for the time I shot the floor in my grandparents' bedroom—but it wasn't my fault!).

The common principle running through all these experiences is the control of gunpowder. When gunpowder ignites, it releases a great deal of energy. If it is just lying on a board out in the open when ignited, all it does is whoosh and hiss— a lot of light, a little noise, and no significant consequences. But if you control the ignition of gunpowder, you can make things happen. In a very primitive way, the matches showed how. When the matches were lit, the aluminum foil forced the release of all the energy in one direction, and a little rocket took off.

IN THIS CHAPTER WE LEARN THAT . . .

1. Episcopalian government is a hierarchical system of governing and decision-making in the church in which denominational leaders are the primary authority.

2. Presbyterian government is a representative system of governing and decision-making in the church in which a board of elders is the primary authority.

3. Congregational government is a democratic system of governing and decision-making in the church in which the congregation as a whole is the primary authority.

This principle is even more obvious with bullets. A common cartridge is made of a small brass cylinder with gunpowder in one end and a lead slug in the other. When the firing pin of the gun hits the end of the cartridge, it causes an explosion in the gunpowder that propels the slug out of the barrel of the gun.

The point? When the release of energy is controlled, you can give direction to it and accomplish things with it.

Driving an automobile depends on the controlled release and direction of energy. Flying to the moon depends on the controlled release and direction of energy. Coaching a basketball team depends on the controlled release and direction of energy. Supervising a day-care center depends on the controlled release and direction of energy. No matter whether it is man or machine, if the release of energy is controlled and directed, positive things can happen. If the release of energy is uncontrolled, explosions happen.

When you get people together in any context, including a church, there is the automatic release of energy. This is inherent in the interaction of people with one another. If you want something positive to happen, rather than an explosion, the energy must be harnessed and directed, which requires organization.

WHY I NEED TO KNOW THIS

I need to know this so that I can evaluate whether or not my church is being governed in a wise manner. Also, I will be able to see that, even if I prefer my own system of church government, I can respect a church that uses another system. I will learn that it is the spiritual maturity of the people that determines how well a system works. There is no magic in any one way of governing. Immature or unscrupulous people can corrupt any system.

From the earliest days of the existence of the church, it got organized. In Acts 6, during the infancy of the church, the new Christians were having some difficulty with meeting the needs of some of the members. So, the apostles instructed the people to choose spiritually mature men to solve the problem. They got organized and the problem was solved. When the apostle Paul planted churches among the Gentiles, one of the first things he did was appoint elders to lead the churches (Acts 14:23; Titus 1:5). The churches got organized and positive things happened. Whenever a few people get together for practically any reason, they have to get organized, and the church is no exception.

Bruce Shelley wrote:

> All life on earth seems to require some sort of form. It is tough to think of formless life. Even a jellyfish has a basic shape. Certainly, in human affairs spirit must express itself in visible structures before it can make a contribution to the ongoing drama of history.

Lost men must hear the Gospel, so adequately trained witnesses must be sent. The meaning of the Gospel for life must be taught to those who believe, so some form of Christian education must be provided. Christians should express the unity of their faith, so some means of public worship must be developed. The unfortunate and needy must be cared for, so some channels for ministry must be created. In short, if the will of Christ, in even the slightest sense, is to be done on this earth as it is in heaven, the church must be organized in some objective form to manifest itself in those areas in which people live out their lives. (*The Church*, 48–49)

The organizational structure of the first churches in Scripture was very simple, but during the last two thousand years, as culture and circumstances have changed, three different approaches to organizing and governing a church have evolved: Episcopalian government, Presbyterian government, and Congregational government.

The correctness of the proper form of church government has been hotly debated over the years, yet each tradition claims biblical support for its approach. Since there is reasonable biblical evidence for each form, perhaps the Lord has given the universal church the freedom to decide how it wishes to govern itself within individual local churches. In fact, while there is no way to prove it, perhaps the reason we see biblical support for each of the three forms of government is because the seeds of each of the three forms is seen in different instances in Scripture. In any event, even though we may think our approach is best, we can respect those who hold to a different one.

For the rest of the chapter, we will look more closely at the three different approaches.

WHAT IS EPISCOPALIAN GOVERNMENT?

Episcopalian government is a hierarchical system of governing and decision-making in the church in which denominational leaders are the primary authority.

Not all churches that operate by the Episcopalian system belong to the Episcopalian denomination. The name comes from the fact that the system emphasizes the role of bishops (from the Greek word *episcopos*, translated "bishop"). Roman Catholics, Eastern Orthodox, and the Church of England, as well as Episcopalians and some Methodists and Lutherans, which together make up the majority of professing Christians in the world, follow this system of church government.

In this system the chief ministers of the church are bishops who have authority over the churches in different geographic regions. Below them are the pastors or priests of the individual churches, and below them are deacons.

In some of the churches, a larger governing body made up of all the bishops has authority over the individual bishops. In the Roman Catholic Church, the bishop of Rome (the pope), of course, has authority over all the other bishops.

Evidence. Those who believe that they see this system in the New Testament point to the apostles, who they believe functioned as bishops over the New Testament churches. Some believe that the apostles passed on to others the authority to be bishops.

As an example, they point to James of Jerusalem, the brother of Jesus, who seemed to be the head of the church in Jerusalem, which would have included many house churches and possibly many pastors. He appeared to have presided over a major council in Jerusalem involving the major leaders of Christianity at the time, playing the role of a bishop (Acts 12:17; 15:13).

As other examples, they point to Timothy and Titus, in the New Testament books that bear their names, as playing a role somewhere between an apostle and the bishops of later times. They both seemed to be involved in appointing elders to oversee churches in their areas, which was later a function of bishops.

It is believed that Jesus' apostles ordained some men, the first bishops, and authorized them to ordain other bishops. Some (especially Roman Catholics and Eastern Orthodox) believe that in doing so they provided for the historic succession of bishops to govern the church in the whole world in succeeding generations, with their authority for doing so being traceable directly back to the apostles themselves. Others who practice Episcopalian government do not believe it is necessary to be able to trace their bishops back to the apostles.

The first churches after the days of the New Testament appear to have functioned this way. Very early Christian writings (second century) reveal this form of government to be in existence in Asia Minor (modern Turkey), ancient Gaul, and North Africa. Soon after, it was seen nearly universally throughout the early church as soon as there were enough writings for us to know how churches functioned. The reasonable conclusion that is drawn from this information is that this form of government is the original and correct form of church government.

Objections. There are objections to this position, however. First, there is no conclusive evidence that bishops were different from elders in New Testament times. The words appear to be interchangeable. If that actually is the case, then bishops have no biblical authority over elders. They are the same thing, perhaps with the word *bishop* tending to be used when addressing Gentile audiences and the word *elder* tending to be used when addressing Jewish audiences.

Second, it is going too far to say that all the ministry of those times was apostolic in origin or under apostolic authority. Perhaps some or even most of the early churches functioned this way, but the question is far from answered as to whether the Lord intended all churches for all time to function this way.

Observations.

1. Whether or not you believe all churches should be episcopalian or not, it cannot be disputed that this form of government appeared very early in the history of the church and was practically universal for hundreds of years.

2. In 1054, there were bishops presiding over churches in most of the world that either directly or indirectly touched Jerusalem. The bishop of Rome proclaimed himself to be the unique successor to Peter, who they understood to be the first bishop, and therefore had the power to pronounce truth as coming from God. Some of the bishops accepted the bishop of Rome's pronouncement and others didn't. Those who did formed the Roman Catholic Church, and those who didn't formed the Eastern Orthodox Church (including the Greek and the Russian Orthodox Churches).

3. Both the Roman Catholic Church and the Eastern Orthodox Church remain episcopal in their church government, and both hold to apostolic succession (the lineage of their bishops can be traced back to the apostles themselves).

4. During the Reformation (A.D. 1517), the organized church in England rejected the authority of the Roman Catholic Church and formed its own church, the Church of England (also known as the Anglican Church), but retained the episcopal church structure that was in existence at the time. So now, the Church of England is presided over by a group of bishops, with a head bishop, the archbishop of Canterbury.

5. While more Christians accept episcopalian government than any other form of church government, episcopally governed churches are not, for the most part, in agreement or communion with each other.

WHAT IS PRESBYTERIAN GOVERNMENT?

Presbyterian government is a representative system of governing and decision-making in the church in which a board of elders is the primary authority.

Not all churches that operate by the presbyterian system are Presbyterian churches, though many (perhaps most) are. This form of government gets its name from the fact that it emphasizes the importance of elders or presbyters (from the Greek word *presbuteros*, translated "elder"). It is clear that elders play a prominent role in the New Testament, but knowing exactly how they functioned in the church is a matter for educated deduction, not clear biblical instructions.

Confusion between this and the previous system seems to stem from differences of opinion as to whether or not elders and bishops are the same thing. The mass of evidence suggests that they are. According to this position, there appears to have been in the Bible a group of elders who formed a kind of committee that was in charge of local church affairs. That is a natural conclusion from passages such as Hebrews 13:17, "Obey those who rule over you, and be submissive, for they watch out for your souls, as those who must give account," and 1 Thessalonians 5:12–13, "Recognize those who labor among you, and are over you in the Lord and admonish you, and to esteem them very highly in love for their work's sake."

From the account of the Council of Jerusalem in Acts 15 we see that the elders occupied an important place at the very highest levels of the early church. In subsequent years church government evolved in such a way that the bishops became more powerful than elders. Perhaps this was because circumstances required strong leaders in times of persecution and early false teaching.

Evidence. The prominence of the ministry of elders in the New Testament is inescapable, and the strongest evidence suggests that bishops and elders are the same thing. If so, there is no biblical basis for giving bishops authority over elders.

Objections. The precise function of elders is not made clear. Therefore, it cannot be assured that the churches in biblical times operated according to a strict presbyterian system.

Observations.

1. To their credit, modern adherents to the presbyterian system do not usually hold that this form of government is the only one in the New Testament. During the Reformation, when Presbyterianism came into prominence, the leaders thought that they were restoring the church to its original system, but few would strongly

defend that position today. They would, however, defend it as a good, and perhaps the best, system today.

2. From the Reformation (approximately A.D. 1500) on, the presbyterian form of government has been a very important and vital viewpoint. It is most commonly found in Presbyterian churches, but is also found in many independent churches.

3. Presbyterian churches (the denomination) are independent of one another. However, they hold in common two major things. First is adherence to church documents such as the Belgic Confession, or Heidelberg Catechism, or the venerable Westminster Confession, and they practice a presbyterial form of church government.

4. Many local congregations are governed by three bodies:

   a. Session—a body made up of a pastor and laypeople from a given church.

   b. Presbytery—a body of teaching and ruling elders from a group of local congregations in a common geographical area who cooperate together.

   c. General Assembly—a denomination-wide body with representatives from individual local churches.

In all such bodies, equality exists between teaching elders (often the pastor) and ruling elders.

WHAT IS CONGREGATIONAL GOVERNMENT?

Congregational government is a democratic system of governing and decision-making in the church in which the congregation as a whole is the primary authority.

The biblical basis for congregational government flows out of several passages. In Colossians 1:18, we read that "He [Christ] is the head of the body," and in 1 Peter 2:9, we read that every believer is a priest. Therefore, we all have direct access to Jesus. We do not have to go through a priest. Anyone who wants to may come to Christ confidently. Therefore, we do not need priests or church authorities over us. Christ is able to be the head of each local congregation.

Added to this direct access to God, which has been given us by the finished work of Christ, are the congregational examples in Scripture. We see independent congregations, not subject to episcopal or presbyterial control. The apostles did exercise a certain authority over local congregations, but that authority passed with the passing of the apostles. Now, there is no room for any absolute human authority.

We see Congregationalism also appearing as a result of the Reformation. In this view, the local congregations were now seen as independent of bishops or magistrates, and each one had the right to function independently, including the right to ordain its own ministers. They viewed bishops and elders as being the same thing, and entrusted each congregation to their ministry. Often, the pastor was seen as the single elder; and a board of laypersons, called deacons, assisted the elder in ministry.

There is a denomination called the Congregational Church that embraces this form of government, as do most Baptists and many independent congregations with no links or affiliations with any denominations.

Evidence. Congregational churches are able to point to New Testament examples in which congregations functioned apparently autonomously (Acts 6:3–5). It applies, in practical corporate ways, the biblical principle of the priesthood of all believers. And it is free of the excesses and distortions of episcopal and presbyterial government.

Objections. Congregationalism does not always reconcile its own position with some of the information in Scripture that could point to the other two types of government. It is subject to the distortions and excesses of independence. And congregational churches sometimes undervalue the benefits of cooperative action and testimony, often feel little heritage with historic Christianity, and can have inadequate appreciation for the traditions and ordinances of the church.

Observations.

1. Congregationalism arose at the same time that democracy began to make itself a force on the world political scene.

2. Authoritarian forms of political government had oppressed the people for hundreds of years, and democracy was a way to escape the political oppression. The same was true of the church. Some churches had done a very poor job of leading the people in spiritual truth, and Congregationalism allowed true Christians to purge themselves of these wrongs very quickly.

3. Congregationalism was not readily accepted in England. There was much political and church opposition to it. As a result, many of these early English Christians emigrated to Holland and then to the United States, where their tastes for democracy were fed, both politically and in their individual local churches.

CONCLUSION

When we look at all the evidence for these three forms of church government, both in the Scripture and in church history, many are left with the impression that it is impossible to conclude that "our" form of government was established by the apostles to the exclusion of any other form of government. It seems prudent to recognize that the New Testament contains seeds of all three forms of church government, each of which could reasonably evolve into these three distinct church forms. While there is solid ground for anyone to feel that his church governing system is good, and perhaps the best, no one has grounds for disrespect of other churches that may function differently. Even if we may have acute doctrinal differences with some churches, that doesn't mean their general form of church government is invalid.

SPEED BUMP!

Slow down to be sure you have gotten the main points of this chapter.

Q1. What is episcopalian government?

A1. Episcopalian government is a *hierarchical* system of governing and decision-making in the church in which denominational leaders are the primary authority.

Q2. What is presbyterian government?

A2. Presbyterian government is a *representative* system of governing and decision-making in the church in which a board of elders is the primary authority.

Q3. What is congregational government?

A3. Congregational government is a *democratic* system of governing and decision-making in the church in which the congregation as a whole is the primary authority.

FILL IN THE BLANK

Q1. What is episcopalian government?

A1. Episcopalian government is a _____ system of governing and decision-making in the church in which denominational leaders are the primary authority.

Q2. What is presbyterian government?

A2. Presbyterian government is a _____ system of governing and decision-making in the church in which a board of elders is the primary authority.

Q3. What is congregational government?

A3. Congregational government is a _____ system of governing and decision-making in the church in which the congregation as a whole is the primary authority.

FOR FURTHER THOUGHT AND DISCUSSION

1. What system of church government are you most familiar with? In your experience, what were the strengths of that system?

2. In your experience, what were the weaknesses of that system?

3. From your experience, what appeals to you about the other two forms of government?

4. What does not appeal to you?

WHAT IF I DON'T BELIEVE?

If we don't believe that church government is necessary, the two alternatives that are very likely are (1) rampant individualism where everyone is free to do whatever is right in his own eyes (which could easily evolve into anarchy), or (2) totalitarianism, where a single pastor has all the authority and calls all the shots. Neither of those are good alternatives.

Each of the three systems of government can work well if it has good people in positions of influence, and each can work very badly if it has the wrong people in positions of influence. We must be sure we are in a church where the leadership is truly spiritually mature, and then the system will probably work.

FOR FURTHER STUDY

1. Scripture

- Acts 12:17
- Acts 15:13
- Colossians 1:18
- 1 Thessalonians 5:12–13
- Hebrews 13:17
- 1 Peter 2:9

WHAT YOU NEED TO KNOW ABOUT THE CHURCH

2. Books

Other books can be helpful in studying this subject further. If I could read only one of these, I would read the first one.

The Church, Bruce Shelley

Know What You Believe, Paul Little

Evangelical Dictionary of Theology, Walter Elwell

10

WHO NEEDS THE CHURCH?

The New Testament does not envisage solitary religion; some kind of regular assembly for worship and instruction is everywhere taken for granted in the Epistles. So we must be regular practicing members of the church.
—C. S. Lewis

When our country was being founded, Benjamin Franklin said of the leaders, referring to the danger of revolting against England, "We must all hang together, or assuredly we shall all hang separately." And so it is. There is strength in unity and numbers. Solomon once said that a cord of one strand was easily broken, but a cord of three strands was not easily broken (Ecclesiastes 4:12).

One of the fundamental tenets of political philosophy is that, in any national government, the "whole" must look out for the welfare of the individual parts, and the individual parts must look out for the welfare of the whole. When this happens, a nation can run smoothly and prosper. I believe this is accurate. It is simply the concept of biblical love applied to government. God has created the world so that, if those in authority commit themselves to the welfare of those under them, and if those under them commit themselves to the welfare of those in authority, everyone will get his needs met in a context of unity and harmony. Love works.

So it is in the church. The Bible makes it clear that those in authority in the church are to look out for the welfare of those they are shepherding (1 Peter 5:1–5) and those in the church are to look out for those in authority (1 Peter 5:6–7). The principle of reciprocal love in the New Testament guides us in the church, and helps us see how the individual needs the church and how the church needs the individual.

Whether it is our need for the church or the church's need for us, we all need each other. If we try to make it alone we "hang" separately. But if we "hang together," we can make it. Our cord alone will be broken, but wound together with all the other cords in the church, we will not be broken.

137

WHY DO INDIVIDUALS NEED THE CHURCH?

Individuals need the church to help them be successful in their personal lives.

In our chapters on "What Should the Church Do," we outlined the responsibilities of the church to the individual. The church should help lead the individual in meaningful worship, provide biblical instruction, encourage fellowship, and equip us for service. However, those were all functional, measurable things. There are other, less measurable reasons why the church is important to us all.

We need the church for a sense of belonging. We were created by God to feel a need to belong to something important and greater than ourselves. Certainly there are other things than the church that are important and greater than ourselves. But the Christian longs to know that what he does is important to God, and that he is doing what God wants him to do. That means he must have some "connection" with the church. Otherwise it would be easy to get lonely and discouraged. If he is involved in a meaningful way with the church, he feels part of a whole. He feels a sense of belonging.

IN THIS CHAPTER WE LEARN THAT . . .

1. Individuals need the church to help them be successful in their personal lives.

2. The church needs individuals to help it be successful in its corporate life.

The twentieth century was the century of the individual. Most, if not all, cultures that we know much about were cultures of "belonging." A person was part of a family, a clan, a people group that had a corporate identity. In the early part of our nation, we identified with being an American. We were proud to be Americans. We felt a "manifest destiny" about ourselves—that we were God's instrument to bring progress, civilization, and freedom to the world. Something has broken down, however. Even families are not really units anymore. They are often nothing more than a collection of individuals living under the same roof. Each has his own bedroom, his own television, his own Walkman, often his own car, his own set of friends, and his own schedule. We all seek to "do our own thing," seek our own pleasure, fulfill our own desires, but we do so at the expense of relationships with others. The more self-determination we gain, the more alienated and lonely we feel, because we jettison relationships for the sake of the right to do what we want to do.

In his book *Who Needs God?*, Harold Kushner has written,

> We might think of it this way: if you are running a marathon just to see if you can do it, if you can will your body to run twenty-six miles, you will enjoy the experience. Your legs will ache and your feet will be blistered, but you will have the sense

of taking part in an adventure, and the other runners will be your comrades in that adventure, sharing an exhilarating experience that most people will never know. But as soon as it becomes important for you to win that race, it is not fun anymore. Now it becomes a grim, competitive business, and now the other runners are your rivals, no longer your comrades. The result: the loneliness of the long-distance runner. (98)

Whenever we must "win" in order to validate our worth as human beings, other people become either resources to be used in the pursuit of our goals or else obstacles to our goals. They are either commodities or roadblocks.

If we see others as resources or obstacles, we cannot help but be lonely. If we see ourselves as one part of a network, one branch in a fruitful vine, loving, looking out for, and helping others, while others love, look out for, and help us, we find what we cannot get any other way. Belonging. No healthy human being can be happy unless he has adequate, meaningful relationships with others. This will happen only if he lives unselfishly.

WHY I NEED TO KNOW THIS

I need to know this so that I will be willing to invest my life in a worthy church, and so that I will put myself under the ministry of that church.

That is what the church can assure. Yes, some people are able to get some sense of belonging through family or friends. However, that sense of belonging is limited if there is no sense of being linked to God. And a sense of belonging through family or friends used to be more common than it is now. Increasingly, families are failing to function as a harmonious unit and satisfy that sense of belonging. The church has the potential to supply it by functioning as a spiritual family. Even faithful Christians find a strong church to be an indispensable contribution to their spiritual lives because of our inherent need to feel at one with God and with the other children of God.

In a culture that creates alienation, the church can provide belonging. In a culture that encourages competition, the church can provide cooperation. In a culture that fosters individualism, the church can provide a team. The church can provide the ceremonies that draw us together for mutual strength and encouragement during the major experiences of life: births, marriages, funerals. Belonging to a caring community that is linked to God gives us people to share both our joys and sorrows. Our joys are doubled and our sorrows are halved.

The church is just another activity in an already busy schedule unless, spiritually, we become a part of the lives of those who attend—unless they allow us into their lives and we allow them into ours. We must become less occupied with finding people who will dedicate themselves to alleviating our loneliness, and more occupied with dedicating ourselves to alleviating the loneliness of others. When we do, both their loneliness and ours are erased. Suddenly, if it works (and it takes two parties to make it work), we belong.

> Against a culture of alienation, the church offers belonging—to God and to one another.

We need the church for greater safety. A second intangible reason the church is so important to us is that it can provide so much safety for us if we will let it. Too often, people see authority as inhibiting, limiting, restricting. Surely it is, yet not all inhibiting, limiting, and restricting is bad. The chain restricts the dog from running out into the street and getting hit by a car. The fence limits the child from doing the same. The speed limit inhibits the inclination to speed and have an accident.

Many adults often see the church the same way teenagers see their parents, as out-of-touch old fogies who don't want to sin because they lack the strength or imagination. They have forgotten what is fun, or lost the ability to have fun, so they dedicate themselves to trying to keep others from having fun. I remember clearly many restrictions my parents put on me as a teenager that I tolerated, not because I thought they were right, but in spite of the fact that I thought they were unnecessary. Why did I have to be in by midnight? Why did I have to drive the speed limit? Why did I have to let them know where I was all the time?

Many times, even though I kept within the limitations they set for me, I was able to do things that were wrong and completely get away with it. That only vindicated my belief that I was really the one who knew how to run my life, and I smugly tried to figure out how I could do the things I wanted to anyway and still not rile them up. I felt superior. I got what I wanted and made them look foolish (I thought) in the process. It wasn't necessary for them to know that I was superior. I was content in the assurance for myself.

I was lucky. My (true) foolishness never cost me dearly. For example, I used to drive too fast. I used to fly down narrow, ice-dotted, and snow-packed country roads at eighty miles an hour. I was lucky that I never had an accident or never killed anyone. I easily could have.

Now that I am the age my parents were when I was giving them all the grief, I realize that they were wise and I was foolish. I realize there was safety in their restrictions. I realize that the smartest thing I could have done was to put myself under the protection of their limitations.

Teenage years are a kind of insanity, and because a common teenage view is that anyone over thirty is automatically mentally challenged, not only including their parents but *especially* their parents, it is often a futile undertaking to tell them that their parents know best.

However, older-than-teenager church members ought to be able to see the analogy. Just as teenagers would find safety if they were to put themselves under the protection of their parents, so Christians would find safety if they put themselves under the protection of their church.

Of course, we are assuming that the church is a good church and deserving of your confidence. Also, we must assume, as we have said elsewhere, that we do not put total confidence in any human authority. A number of years ago, the world was shocked when a large group of people put their total confidence in their pastor, Jim Jones, who persuaded them all to commit suicide. That is not the kind of confidence and submission to authority we are encouraging. Rather, we are encouraging confidence in and submission to a church that deserves it by virtue of the moral character and spiritual maturity of its leaders, and its commitment to the Scripture. But even then, we always use the Scriptures to evaluate everything that is said and done.

> In a dangerous culture, the church offers sanctuary, the peace of Christ.

If it is a good church and you exercise reasoned submission, there is much protection under the authority of the church. If the church is a Bible-believing church with spiritually mature leadership, the church will not want you to sin sexually, or use your money foolishly, or marry unwisely, or lose control of emotions, or be dishonest, or a hundred other sins you could commit. And all this would be for your benefit. It would protect you from harm.

Many times I have listened to people tell me stories of heartache and tragedy that could have been averted if people had just put themselves under the protection of the church.

WHY DOES THE CHURCH NEED INDIVIDUALS?

The church needs individuals to help it be successful in its corporate life.

The church needs our loyalty and commitment. Loyalty and commitment are wounded virtues. Today, many people care little about them, and those who might care have a diminished capacity for them. The reason? Without the help of culture, many of us have a diminished capacity to see the full picture of loyalty and commitment, and a diminished capacity to want them in our lives as badly as we ought to want them.

For example, the father of a close friend never drove a car in his entire life except an Oldsmobile. If my memory serves me correctly, he owned twenty-seven cars in his seventy-some years, and every one was an Olds. This year it was an Oldsmobile Eighty-eight, and that year it was an Oldsmobile Toronado, but always an Olds. Few of us identify with that kind of loyalty. Perhaps someone might say that blind loyalty is not a virtue but a weakness. I agree. However, a person who has that capacity for loyalty to a car often has a great capacity for loyalty to God and other things we ought to be loyal to.

The difference between loyalty and commitment is that "loyalty" sticks with something, while "commitment" is willing to pay a high price while sticking. My mother and father had six children. I'm the youngest. As a laborer, my father didn't make a lot of money. Almost everyone I knew was better off than we were. But my mother and father were committed to marriage, committed to us children, and committed to paying whatever price was necessary to do what was right.

My father was a fairly young man when he died. He was fifty-four. If he hadn't had six kids, he would have had an easier life, he could have afforded more pleaures, he could have had a higher standard of living. But I don't think those things ever occurred to him. I believe he thought that he was rich with six kids and all the grandchildren they gave him. He left behind six children who know what it is to be committed. And that virtue is cropping up in grandchildren and great-grandchildren. A person who has that capacity for commitment to a family often has a great capacity for commitment to God and other things we ought to be committed to.

I was lucky. When I grew up, the small world in which I lived was filled with people who, merely by living their lives in front of me, taught me a high level of loyalty and commitment. When I look around at the culture today, I see spouses bailing out on spouses, parents bailing out on children, employees bailing out on employers, friends bailing out on friends. Children growing up in this environment have a stunted concept of what loyalty and commitment are, and thus a stunted capacity to live out those virtues.

This is a profound disadvantage, because God calls us to lives of loyalty and commitment to Him. He wants us to be *totally* committed to Him *forever*. Those are the two extremes of commitment and loyalty. God calls us to give our lives to Him as living sacrifices, and to never fail in that commitment (Romans 12:1–2; 1 Corinthians 13:8). If that is true, let me make a link between that fact and the "church."

1. We are called to total and unending loyalty and commitment to God.

2. The church is important to God. In fact, the central thing God is doing in the world today is building His church (Matthew 16:18). There is nothing more important to God right now than the church.

3. Therefore, we cannot claim loyalty to God without offering loyalty to His church.

Of course, we do not offer unconditional loyalty to a local church. The local church is led by and made up of imperfect people, and no human being or institution deserves our unconditional loyalty. However, to the degree that a local church approximates the ideals of the universal church, we are to be loyal to it.

> Loyalty sticks with something, while commitment pays a high price while sticking.

So, how loyal are you to the church? How committed are you to the church? If everyone treated the church the way you do, what shape would the church be in?

I came of age in the sixties. It was a terrible time. Much that was important and valuable to our society collapsed and died in the sixties. I saw it happening around me . . . the sexual revolution, the fall of respect for authority, the rise of selfishness and individualism. Starting with my generation—the first baby boomers—and continuing (and possibly worsening) today, we are not very loyal or committed to the church. We have a consumer mentality toward the church. I am concerned about Me. The most important thing in the world is Me. If I am going to go to church, it is going to be for Me. I want to know what I am going to get out of it. If the church doesn't meet my expectations, I will go down the road to one that does, or I will stay home and watch *Sunday Morning* on TV, drink coffee, eat toasted bagels, and work the *New York Times* crossword puzzle.

This is wrong. Our attitude ought to be, *God deserves my loyalty and commitment. The church is the most important thing in the world to God. Therefore, the church deserves my loyalty and commitment. As a result, I must find the local church that comes closest to promoting the ideals of the universal church and commit myself to it.*

You will not find a perfect local church. If you find one that is, don't join it. You'll ruin it. But join the best imperfect one you can find. We should all do what we can to help make the church all that it should be. We should make sure that if everyone treats our church the way we do, the church will thrive.

The church needs our resources. If the church deserves our loyalty and commitment, what do we do?

The answer is that we manifest our heart by "giving." The Bible says that God so *loved* the world that He *gave* His only Son for us (John 3:16). It admonishes husbands to love their wives as Christ also *loved* the church and *gave* Himself up for it (Ephesians 5:25). Throughout the Bible, we see that love doesn't take; it gives (1 Corinthians 13:4–7). If we are going to love what God loves—if we are going to love the church—we must give to it. What do we give? Ourselves first, but then we give of our resources as a result of having given ourselves (2 Corinthians 8:5). We all have resources that the church must have if it is to thrive.

> Anyone who works his head off without praying has mixed-up theology.

We all have time. Each of us has twenty-four hours in a day. Certainly we are all busy. I don't know of many people who aren't busy. So we cannot give the church our leftover time. We don't have any. We must make the church a priority, and if we don't currently have enough time for it, we must reevaluate how we're spending our time and drop something that is of lesser priority.

How much time? That is between you and the Lord. But your conscience must be clear about it. It will take some time. Ask Him to direct you.

We all have talents. Each of us is gifted to do something. Each of us has been gifted by God with a spiritual gift, and that gift is to be used for the benefit of others (Ephesians 4:16; 1 Peter 4:10). What should we do? That is between you and the Lord. But your conscience must be clear about it. You are to use your talents and gifts for Him. Ask Him to direct you.

We all have treasure. God has enabled each of us to make money. Some have very little money, and some have a lot of money, but each of us is to give to the Lord as He has prospered us. If we have very little money, He may only expect a little money from us, but it will be considered great treasure (Mark 14:42). If we have a lot of money, He may expect a lot of money from us, and it will only be considered a great treasure if it is truly a lot of money.

How much money? That is between you and the Lord. But your conscience must be clear about it. You have money, and you are to give to His work as He has prospered you. Ask Him to direct you.

A lack of resources for local churches is often a reflection of a lack of loyalty and commitment, at least in a wealthy country like the United States. To get more resources for ministry, the church must address the lack of loyalty and commitment to God and His priorities. When priorities are where they need to be, the resources God wants for ministry will often fall into place.

We all can pray. We are given the privilege of praying to God. In fact, we are commanded to pray (1 Thessalonians 5:17). Someone said, "Let's have a word of prayer before we get down to work." Someone else responded, "The prayer *is* the work."

If it is true that everything accomplished in the world of a spiritual nature is done by God (John 15:5), then it is inescapable that we ought to pray. It is fruitless for us to work without praying (Psalm 127:1). When we share the gospel, we do not speak with people who are blindfolded, who need only to be implored to take off their blindfold. Rather, we are speaking with those who are blind (2 Corinthians 4:4). And we need to implore the God of heaven to break through the darkness and help them see. In evangelism, prayer is the work.

When we minister to Christians, we do not minister to people who, without God working in us (Philippians 2:13), are able to transform themselves into the character image of God and need only to be implored to do so. Rather, we minister to people who are helpless to understand and apply Scripture (1 Corinthians 2:9—3:7) and change into the character image of Christ (Galatians 5:19–23). So we need to implore the God of heaven to help His children see the truth of Scripture and to transform them into the character image of Christ. In all ministry, prayer is the work.

If you see someone working his head off without praying, he has mixed-up theology. He doesn't understand what he is doing. He thinks he can do the work of God. He cannot. He should first pray.

We all can give goodwill. Each of us communicates loudly and clearly what we think of something. We cannot avoid doing so. We communicate not only by what we say and do, but by what we don't say and don't do. That is why we cannot avoid communicating what we really think and feel. We need to give the church our goodwill. People will know if we do and if we don't. Don't give your time, talents, treasure, and prayer to the church with a bad attitude. Ask God to change you. Then you won't infect anyone else with your condition. Then you can serve with the spirit of Christ, being more concerned with giving than receiving. Then you can jump in and give *of* yourself, and you'll be giving *yourself* to the thing that God thinks is the most important thing in the world right now, His church.

CONCLUSION

The church and individual Christians must live in a symbiotic relationship. They need each other. The individual needs the church for a sense of belonging, for guidance, direction, and safety. The church is a spiritual mother to the individual Christian, yet we often live like orphans. Conversely, the church needs the individual. It needs the loyalty, commitment, physical resources, and spiritual resources. The church and the individual need each other, and neither will be healthy without the other.

SPEED BUMP!

Slow down to be sure you have gotten the main points of this chapter.

Q1. Why do individuals need the church?

A1. Individuals need the church to help them be successful in their *personal* lives.

Q2. Why does the church need individuals?

A2. The church needs individuals to help it be successful in its *corporate* life.

FILL IN THE BLANK

Q1. Why do individuals need the church?

A1. Individuals need the church to help them be successful in their _____ lives.

Q2. Why does the church need individuals?

A2. The church needs individuals to help it be successful in its _____ life.

FOR FURTHER THOUGHT AND DISCUSSION

1. What in your experience has been the greatest benefit you have received from your relationship with a church? How do you think that benefit could be experienced by even more people?

2. What has been the greatest problem you have experienced in your relationship with a church? How do you think that problem could be overcome so that others don't experience it?

3. What do you think the church's greatest potential benefit is from your involvement? What is the greatest actual benefit it has experienced from your involvement? What do you think you could/should do to be a more biblical church attender?

WHAT IF I DON'T BELIEVE?

If I don't believe that I need the church and the church needs me, I am not likely to pay the personal price to give of myself to the church, and I am not likely to allow the church to minister to my needs. The church loses (meaning other people lose) and I lose.

FOR FURTHER STUDY

1. Scripture

- Matthew 16:18
- John 3:16
- Romans 12:1–2
- 1 Corinthians 13:4–8
- Ephesians 5:25
- 1 Peter 4:10

2. Book

The Body, Charles Colson

11

HOW SHOULD THE CHURCH STAND AGAINST THE WORLD?

The church is against the world, for the world.
—Hartford Declaration, 1975

Throughout Scripture, the kingdoms of this world and the kingdom of God are continually being contrasted. Some slick lawyers were trying to trip up Jesus and get Him to say something they could hold against Him, so they asked Him if they should pay taxes to Caesar or not. The trick was that if He said yes, they could accuse Him of saying we should serve or worship someone other than God. They didn't trip Him.

Jesus asked them to get a coin. They did. He asked whose image was on it. They said, "Caesar's." Jesus said, "Render therefore to Caesar the things that are Caesar's [taxes], and to God the things that are God's [our personal worship]" (Matthew 22:21).

The kingdoms of the world are temporal. The kingdom of God is eternal. The kingdoms of the world are physical. The kingdom of God is spiritual. The kingdoms of the world are "eating and drinking" (Romans 14:17). The kingdom of God is "righteousness." The Christian is to be in the world but not of the world. He is to treat the world as a sinking ship. Rather than putting all his hopes and dreams in this world, he puts his hopes and dreams in the next world (1 John 2:15–17).

The Christian has two jobs in this world: to encourage as many people as possible to get into the lifeboat before the ship sinks, and to help make the ship as good a place as he can while it is still afloat. We do not abandon the ship to the rats. We treat it as God's creation, and try to bring kingdom principles to bear while the ship still floats.

149

One of the great challenges of the Christian life is to live in this world with the values of the next (Colossians 3:1–4). We tend to live in this world with the values of this world, and it is a continuous, until-we-die struggle.

Comedian Bill Cosby has a routine in which he describes the time he got his tonsils taken out as a child. He asked the doctor why he had to have his tonsils taken out. The doctor said it was because his tonsils were supposed to stand guard at the door of his throat and not let any germs in. If any germs tried to get in, the tonsils were supposed to trap the germs and kill them. "However," the doctor said, "your tonsils are not doing their job. In fact, they have *joined the other side* and are actually adding germs to your body. So, they gotta go."

Perhaps the single greatest problem in the church today is that, when it comes to their values and lifestyle, many Christians, like bad tonsils, have joined the other side. Instead of standing with the church against the world, they are trying to stand with one foot in the church and one in the world. This divided loyalty keeps them from truly enjoying the church and from positively influencing the world.

The church is to be a countercultural force in the world. This does not mean we are to wear plain clothes, go without electricity, and drive horses and buggies instead of cars. There is nothing wrong with doing that, but that is not what it means to be "counterculture." To be counterculture for the Christian means that we stand against the ungodly values of the world. The world worships and serves self. The kingdom worships and serves God. The world follows desire. The kingdom follows truth. The world takes. The kingdom gives. The world seeks pleasure. The kingdom seeks service.

Whatever lifestyle choices we are faced with in our culture, we should do what we do because it is our way of standing for the church against the world.

WHY I NEED TO KNOW THIS

I need to know this because otherwise I may not be clear on issues of right and wrong, and may fail to take a stand for the kingdom when I should.

I want to be sure I do not miscommunicate. We are not against the world in the sense of being hostile or antagonistic to it. Rather we are against the world in the sense that we do not embrace its fundamental values (rejecting God, being the primary one). We fight against the encroachment of the values of the world into the church. Being against the world does not mean we get out of politics. It means we get into politics. Being against the world does not mean we get out of education. It means we get into education. Being against the world does not mean we get out of

> **The church is against the world, for the world.**

the arts. It means we get into them. We infiltrate every legitimate area of human life. But when we get there, we act and make decisions based on kingdom values, not worldly values.

There are countless ways the church needs to stand against the world (1 Corinthians 16:13). The ones I mention are not all of them. They are just some of the important ones, and they will help us see other ways of standing for eternal values in a temporal world.

WHAT IS THE "KINGDOM STAND" ON RACE?

The "kingdom stand" on race is that all people are created equal
in the sight of God, and all discrimination is sin.

The issue of racial discrimination for the Christian is a simple one. Jesus said, "Do to others what you would have them do to you" (Matthew 7:12 NIV). In this spirit, Abraham Lincoln said, "As I would not be a slave, so I would not be a master." If you would not like to have others discriminate against you, then it is a sin for you to discriminate against them. Period. There is no more room for discussion. All discrimination is sin, whether it is white against black, Hispanic against Asian, rich white against poor white, Protestant against Catholic, or the other way around on all those issues. James made it clear that all people are created equal in the sight of God, that there is no discrimination with God, and there is to be no partiality with His children (2:1–13).

We are currently undergoing a radical evolution in the United States in which Caucasians are gradually becoming a smaller percentage of the total population. Sociologists refer to it as the "coloring of America." Blacks, Hispanics, and Asians are rapidly combining to outnumber whites in many major metropolitan centers. With the long history of race difficulties between whites and blacks, and with the ethnic differences that exist within the Asian-American community, not to say others, the coloring of America could present one of the major sociological problems of the twenty-first century. If we are to thrive as a nation, we must learn to get along together, and if anyone is going to lead the way in getting along together, it should be the church. If Christians cannot demonstrate what it means to be color-blind, who will? America needs our leadership, but the church needs to lead for its own sake too, if it is going to stand against the world with eternal values.

How should we lead? First, by making sure there is no discrimination in our own hearts. Second, by getting together with all other Christians and asking the Lord to show the church how to model the true brotherhood of humanity. There are a million ways to lead, but none of them will work unless our hearts are color-blind.

WHAT IS THE "KINGDOM STAND" ON ABORTION?

The "kingdom stand" on abortion is that human life is sacred, and the taking of innocent human life is a sin.

A medical doctor once told me that I ought to eat two eggs every day (I have no cholesterol problems whatsoever). I asked him why. He said, "Because there is everything in an egg that is needed to make a whole chicken." Therefore, it provides the human body with complete nutrition.

Likewise there is everything in a human embryo to make an adult person. The embryo *is* a whole person waiting to grow up. Nothing except nutrition is added to the embryo from the moment of conception until that person dies of old age.

The historic tradition on abortion for the Roman Catholic Church, the Eastern Orthodox Church, and Protestant churches has been in favor of the sanctity of human life and against abortion. Since the 1973 Supreme Court decision (*Roe v. Wade*) made abortion legal in the United States, many churches have adopted a pro-abortion stand.

We have been created by God in His image (Genesis 1:26–27). Therefore, human life is sacred. Exodus 20:21–25 indicates that God views the unborn child as a human life (see the New King James Version for the clearest translation of this passage). God also commands against the taking of innocent life (Exodus 20:13). Since abortion is the taking of innocent human life, it is a sin.

It would take a large volume dedicated solely to this subject to present all the evidence in favor of a pro-life position. (For further study see "Books" at the end of this chapter.) In this volume, I present the simple pro-life statement that all human life is sacred, even unborn human life, and that it is the obligation of the Christian to stand against abortion and in favor of all innocent human life. The book of Proverbs says, "Deliver those who are being taken away to death, and those who are staggering to slaughter, O hold them back. If you say, 'See, we did not know this,' . . . does He not know it who keeps your soul? And will He not render to man according to his work?" (24:11–12 NASB).

How should you stand against it? God calls each of us to different levels of involvement, so each person must ask that question of the Lord. But the very least a person can do is be clear about his or her own position, and take whatever opportunities we can to support the sanctity of human life. Since the *Roe v. Wade* decision became the law of the land, lives have been taken of enough children to populate the cities of Seattle, Portland, San Francisco, San Diego, Las Vegas, Phoenix, Salt Lake City, Denver, Dallas, Fort Worth, Houston, San Antonio, New Orleans, St. Louis, Minneapolis, Milwaukee, Indianapolis, Detroit, Cleveland, Philadelphia, Boston, Baltimore, Nashville, Atlanta, and Orlando.

What if we were to wipe out the populations of those cities? On what scale could we calculate the tragedy? It is incalculable. Yet, because we never see these lives, we let the tragedy go on.

> All human life is sacred, even unborn human life, and the church must stand against any taking of innocent human life.

Those who have been involved in an abortion need not carry around ongoing guilt about it. Forgiveness is available from the Lord. Repentance is the beginning of healing. We need not live our lives looking backward. But as we look forward, if we are to take a "kingdom stand" against the world, we must uphold the sanctity of human life, and do what the Lord calls us to do to protect innocent human life, including the unborn.

WHAT IS THE "KINGDOM STAND" ON SEXUAL PURITY?

The "kingdom stand" on sexual purity is that
sexual activity outside of marriage is sin.

It does not matter whether the issue is premarital sex, homosexuality, adultery, incest, or bestiality; all sexual activity outside of heterosexual marriage is sin (Leviticus 18:6–12, 23; 1 Corinthians 6:9, 18). Again, this has been the historic stand of all churches, Catholic, Orthodox, and Protestant, until the sexual revolution of the sixties in America. Since then, the increasingly permissive standards toward sexual behavior by society in general have begun to be reflected in the church. Today, we face two major problems. One is Christians who have "joined the other side," holding to a lower standard for sexual purity than the Bible does. The other is Christians who claim the same standard of sexual purity that the Bible does, but who do not have the self-control to live up to their own (and the Bible's) standards.

Christians must take a stand against the world by holding forth values, taking seriously the scriptural teaching on sexual purity, and embracing scriptural standards as their own. Also, those who do not have the self-discipline necessary to live up to them must find some way to get the help necessary to do so. Perhaps a spiritual accountability relationship with a more mature Christian or other prudent steps could be taken to help the Christian live up to scriptural standards. (See "Books" at the end of this chapter.)

WHAT IS THE "KINGDOM STAND" ON FASHION?

The "kingdom stand" on fashion is that clothing
that may identify us as ungodly is unacceptable.

Fashion is often neutral, but not always. When I was in college, the first miniskirt craze swept the fashion world. It was next to impossible for a woman to find a dress or skirt that wasn't scandalously short. A woman could not sit down without imperiling her modesty. Yet, Christian men were not supposed to look at their legs or have any dishonoring thoughts. We all had to pretend that nothing was amiss. There was a sort of silent agreement not to say, "My word, that dress is short! Don't you want something to cover up your lap?" It was a ridiculous situation.

Christians ought to dress in a manner that reflects our commitment to holiness. This means we should not dress in a manner that tempts others to sin, or demeans us or dishonors God. With this in mind, we must also evaluate not only our clothes, but also our overall appearance. There were certain fashions in Bible times that, apparently, only morally loose women followed (1 Corinthians 11:5–6).

The Corinthian women who appeared in the assembly without the head-covering were actually putting themselves on the low level of the temple prostitutes. The prostitutes wore their hair very short, and they did not wear a head-covering in public. Their hairstyle and manner announced to others just what they were and what they were offering.

In Jewish law, a woman proved guilty of adultery had her hair cut off (Numbers 5:11–31) (Warren Wiersbe, *The Bible Exposition Commentary*, 1:604).

So the Bible cautioned women of that day not to look like prostitutes. Using that principle, it seems reasonable to say that we should not identify with ungodliness in our appearance.

There are three broad principles I think we ought to keep in mind as we evaluate which fashions are harmless and which ones are not.

First is the principle of *modesty* (1 Timothy 2:9). Does the clothing we wear make a sensual statement, or entice the opposite sex? If so, it is inappropriate.

Second is the principle of *identification* (1 Corinthians 11:5–6; 1 Thessalonians 5:22). Does any fashion, whether it is clothing, jewelry, hair, or anything else identify us with a godless value system? Would it be appropriate for Christians to wear anything that identified them with satanism, witchcraft, or voodoo?

Third is the principle of *mutilation* (1 Kings 18:25–28; 1 Thessalonians 5:22). Does the fashion involve physical disfiguring or mutilation? Tribes that are given over to demonization often mutilate the body. Sometimes, they split their lips or noses or ears and insert sticks or bones or little plates, and keep enlarging them until huge articles can be placed in the ears, lips, or nose. In other tribes, when children reach puberty, they smash and chip out their teeth. Others lavishly tattoo the entire body. While I can't prove it, I believe that this mutilation of the body may be a demonically energized practice (1 Kings 18:25–28; 1 Corinthians 10:19–20).

> Our physical appearance must be modest, clearly identifying us with that which is good, and free from bodily mutilation.

In the United States, now, we are seeing an increase in fashions that mutilate the body. Many people now wear so many earrings that their ear is permanently disfigured. Some wear not just modest nose rings but many nose rings, some being large, permanently disfiguring the nose. In addition, it is becoming increasingly popular to wear rings and other devices in other parts of the body, such as through the arm or through the belly button. No one can say when you cross the line from a modestly pierced ear to body mutilation, but at some point the line is crossed, and I believe it is wrong.

The body of the Christian is the temple of the Holy Spirit (1 Corinthians 6:19), who moves people to keep the body clean, healthy, and natural, as God created it. I believe it is demonic to allow the body to be dirty, to be unhealthy, and to be mutilated; and when a culture accepts filth, self-destruction, and mutilation of the body, I believe it is a sign of encroaching demonic influence on that culture.

By no means do I believe that each person who is dirty or willfully unhealthy (drugs, alcohol, tobacco, etc.) is also demon-possessed. I do not. Rather, I mean the fashion is one inspired and encouraged by demons. Whenever a society encourages demonization, these practices will increase. I believe this observation is strengthened not only by looking at primitive tribes, but also by observing that these influences started in America in the rock, drug, and occult subcultures, which appear to have strong demonic influence.

Certainly, there is no one "Christian" appearance. There are businesspeople and politicians who have neat, carefully groomed hair, wear crisp blue suits, and have spit-polished shoes who are greedy and corrupt. And there are people who dress like Hell's Angels who are deeply committed Christians, who sometimes continue to dress as they do in order to minister to others in that subculture. Probably no matter how you dress, there are going to be others who dress the same way who do not share Christian values.

Fashion changes start small and progress slowly so that there is often no line of demarcation that says, "This side of the line is okay and that side of the line isn't." However, there are some fashion statements that are not in keeping with a Christian value system, and ought not to be made by Christians.

Of course, most of us do not have trouble seeing the extremes. It is the gray area in the middle that is troublesome. But if we follow the principle of dressing in a way that sincerely, before God, emphasizes our commitment to holiness, rather than our commitment to being fashionable or identifying with a group of people who clearly do not share holy values, we will not do a disservice to ourselves, others, or God.

WHAT IS THE "KINGDOM STAND" ON ENTERTAINMENT?

The "kingdom stand" on entertainment is that we will entertain ourselves only with those things that do not damage our progress toward holiness.

Many of the same problems that plague Christians in the area of fashion also plague us in the area of entertainment. The entertainment values of the world have fallen into the basement since the mid-sixties. We are in a moral freefall as a nation, and the nation is taking many Christians with it. Before the mid-sixties, television generally did not reflect ungodly values. Then, it got so bad that many of the television programs could not be watched by sensitive Christians. Now, if you find an occasional decent program, the commercials and advertisements for future programing are so bad you can't watch the decent programs.

Movies also are cesspools of violence, sex, vulgar language, the occult, and general godlessness. Popular music is dominated with themes of sex, violence, rebellion, and self-gratification. As a nation, we have a hunger and thirst for self-destructive entertainment. In a front-page editorial in my hometown newspaper this morning, the headline is "We Truly Love Our Sex and Violence." The editorial proceeds to decry the values of modern media.

Like the frog in water, we have boiled slowly until we accept as normal much entertainment that would have been unthinkable before the sexual revolution of the sixties. And the church, even though it may be a few years behind, has tended to slide down the same slippery slope as the world, instead of standing firm against the world.

> **Entertainment that is Christian will not damage, but encourage our pursuit of holiness.**

Yet, the apostle Paul wrote, "Whatever is true, whatever is honorable, whatever is right, whatever is pure, whatever is lovely, whatever is of good repute, if there is any excellence and if anything worthy of praise, dwell on these things" (Philippians 4:8 NASB). In another letter, he wrote, "Do not participate in the unfruitful deeds of darkness, but instead even expose them; for it is disgraceful even to speak of the things which are done by them in secret" (Ephesians 5:11–12 NASB). If it is disgraceful even to speak of those things, how much more disgraceful is it to bring them into our homes and watch them! David wrote, "I will walk within my house with a perfect heart. I will set nothing wicked before my eyes" (Psalm 101:2–3). If we were to filter our entertainment through these verses, it would change dramatically the entertainment that many Christians allow themselves.

If we take a "kingdom stand" against the world in our entertainment, we will not entertain ourselves with things that damage our pursuit of holiness.

WHAT IS THE "KINGDOM STAND" ON POLITICAL INVOLVEMENT?

The "kingdom stand" on political involvement is that Christians are obligated to support justice and righteousness in their political decisions.

Each of us is called to differing levels of political involvement. However, each of us, I believe, is obligated to fulfill the basic responsibility to vote. And in our voting, we are responsible to support justice and righteousness.

According to the Bible, the responsibility of kings in the Old Testament was to establish justice and righteousness in the land (2 Samuel 8:15; Psalm 33:5; Isaiah 5:7; Jeremiah 22:3; Amos 5:24). The economic, military, and social welfare of the nation depended on its righteousness. I believe the same is basically true today. We are not promised direct divine blessing in return for righteousness as Israel was in the Old Testament, but righteousness results in blessings in a cause-and-effect way. If we are moral, honest, hardworking, chaste, and ethical, our economy, military, education system, and so forth will flourish. If we are immoral, dishonest, lazy, and unethical, everything begins to break down. Unrighteousness results in curses in a cause-and-effect way.

In the Old Testament, kings had the ability to influence justice and righteousness to a great degree, since they had virtually absolute power. God's blessing came or departed from the nation, depending on the national righteousness, which depended on the king's righteousness.

> **Today, each is to vote as if his vote determined the nation's destiny.**

Today, we do not have kings in America. Instead, we live in a democratic republic in which each citizen has a vote. Therefore, in casting our vote, each of us is responsible to vote as though we were a king and our vote would determine the destiny of the nation. In our vote, our primary concern, if the principle in the Old Testament is true, is to uphold justice and righteousness in the land, not primarily the economy, or foreign policy, or domestic policy. If we have basically competent people running for office, it is important that these basically competent people support just and righteous government.

There are Christians who vote for unrighteous people for political office because of their stand on economic issues, or military issues, or educational issues. Yet if these politicians are immoral people who not only will not help establish justice and righteousness in the land, but actually promote the opposite, we have made a mistake. Christians are such a large percentage of the population in the United States that if all of us voted for issues of justice and righteousness first and political issues second, we would be able to influence profoundly our progress toward greater justice and righteousness in America.

To be clear, I do not believe that we can elect righteous but incompetent people. To elect a spiritually sincere but incompetent person to the presidency would be disastrous. But of all the people running for office who are politically competent, we must vote for those who will most faithfully advance justice and righteousness. Not only must we vote for those who run, but some of us should perhaps be encouraging the right people to run and assisting them. In fact, some of us ourselves may need to run.

WHAT IS THE "KINGDOM STAND" ON THE DISADVANTAGED?

*The "kingdom stand" on the disadvantaged is that we ought
to help those who cannot help themselves.*

Widows and orphans in biblical times were particularly disadvantaged. If someone did not help them, the consequences could be disastrous. The Bible makes it clear that widows and orphans are at the top of God's list of those we need to care for (Isaiah 10:1–2; James 1:27). Of course, in our complicated society today, there are many more who are disadvantaged and need our help. We must help them. Charles Colson and the ministry he founded, Prison Fellowship, has made a dramatic impact on prison ministries around the world, because he is committed to helping the disadvantaged in prison, and their families. The poor, the homeless, the mentally impaired, the physically challenged are all people who need our help.

This does not mean that disadvantaged people have a right to act irresponsibly, or that we have an obligation to pay for people's irresponsibility. In the Bible, widows in the church were to be supported, but only if they met certain requirements of personal responsibility (1 Timothy 5:3–11). People who were out of work could receive help, but only if they were willing to work for the help they received (2 Thessalonians 3:10). We do not help people if we simply give them a handout. We must insist on responsible behavior, but with that behavior we must help them.

WHAT IS THE "KINGDOM STAND" ON THE CHURCH?

*The "kingdom stand" on the church is that the church is primarily in the "righteousness"
business, and anytime another agenda supersedes that one, it has left its reason for existence.*

The church exists to worship God, build up believers, and evangelize the world. Anytime the church adopts another agenda, it has lost the very justification of its existence. If the church is tempted to focus primarily on social commentary, it becomes inferior to the major newsmagazines, newspapers, and electronic media. If the church is tempted to focus primarily on social programs, it becomes inferior to social agencies. If the church is tempted to focus primarily on political involvement, it becomes inferior to political action committees. If the church is tempted to become a social club, it becomes inferior to country clubs. There is nothing the church can do better than anyone else except worship God, build up Christians, and evangelize the world.

That does not mean the church should not engage in social commentary, or social programs, or political involvement. When moral issues are at stake, the church is not only free to become involved in those things, it is obligated to become involved. However, when those things take center stage in the life of the church, the church is out of balance.

WHAT IS THE "KINGDOM STAND" ON EVANGELISM?

The "kingdom stand" on evangelism is that each Christian must accept personal responsibility for involvement in the Great Commission.

The Great Commission, in Matthew 28:19–20, is the mandate to take the message of salvation to the ends of the earth. If you are a Christian, try to envision what your life would be like if you had never heard the gospel. Commonly, we envision that our lives would be shipwrecked if not for Christ on earth, *and* we would be in jeopardy of eternal condemnation. After you envision how dreadful it would be for you not to have become a Christian, then envision how dreadful it is for other people who have never heard.

> God calls us to different levels of evangelism, but all are called to be involved.

Each of us needs to make a personal commitment to the Great Commission, to do what we can to further the cause of taking the gospel to the whole world. Some of us may dedicate our lives to foreign missions. Others of us may concentrate on evangelistic ministry near home. Others of us may concentrate on other kinds of ministry, but commit ourselves to supporting with our finances and prayers those who have a ministry of evangelism, and to working toward opportunities to share our faith through our church, at work, in our neighborhood, and with our family. God will call each of us to different levels of evangelism, but each of us must be committed and involved. Each of us must have a clear conscience before God that we are doing what He wants us to do in the area of evangelism.

The world would like to intimidate us into silence, and for many of us it's working. Too many of us are chameleons in the world. We try to fit in. We try not to be conspicuous. We try to be accepted. We don't want to say anything that will make another person uncomfortable or make ourselves look weird. However, when we are committed to remaining invisible and silent Christians, we violate God's commandments, we miss out on rich blessings ourselves, and others who need to hear the gospel from us don't.

160

Let me illustrate that last point in the hope that it will encourage you to look for opportunities to share your faith. I used to minister with an organization that taught the Bible to Christians. One day a pastor challenged those of us in that ministry to share the gospel during our one-day teaching seminars. We explained patiently to this pastor that these were not evangelistic seminars. They were Bible-teaching seminars aimed at those who were already Christians. The pastor continued: "You are teaching the Bible all day long to crowds that are large enough that they have to have non-Christians in them. The power of the Word is such that there are bound to be people in those seminars who want to become Christians as a result of what they are hearing, and you are not giving them a chance."

So, we decided to give it a shot. We decided that for the next year, we would include a ten-minute explanation of the gospel toward the end of the day and invite anyone who was not a Christian to become one. One year later, five thousand people had come to Christ! That pastor was right. There are people out there who want to know more about spiritual things, who want to know more about God and the Bible, who want to know what truth is and how to live. You are not giving them a chance if you are committed to silence, for "How then shall they call on Him in whom they have not believed? And how shall they believe in Him of whom they have not heard? And how shall they hear without a preacher?" (Romans 10:14).

Agreed, there is no virtue in beating people over the head with a Bible who are not interested in talking about it. But if you remain sensitive to opportunities, tossing out careful comments or asking concerned questions from time to time that people can pick up on, God will give you opportunities to tell other people your story of salvation through Christ. It may bring them to theirs. Those of us in the church need to stand against the world's desire to silence us.

CONCLUSION

These issues are certainly not the only areas in which the church needs to stand against the world. If you had been writing this chapter, you might have left some of these out and added others. But I thought that by going through these, we could see some important areas, and also get ideas on how we need to stand against the world in other areas.

It seems to me that we need to do two things. First, we need to make up our minds. We need to decide what is right and wrong and why. Many people don't have clearly identified ideas of right and wrong. Some time back, some people in our church were discussing the problem of young Christian girls getting pregnant out of wedlock. One of the people in the group said in a compassionate and consoling voice, "Well, the problem with young people today is that they just love each other too much too soon." Without being harsh, but being clear on the truth, such pregnancies are not a result of loving each other too much too soon. Rather, they are a result of not loving each other enough. They are a result of lust getting inflamed to the point that it overtakes love. Because of lust, people commit fornication and get into a real mess of their own making that the Bible could have saved them from if they had trusted and obeyed it.

We must be clear on what is right and what is wrong.

Second, we must take a stand for what is right, not in some obnoxious, overbearing way, but in an enlightened and sensitive way. We can do that in big ways when we get the opportunity, but usually we do it in a thousand little ways: a quiet word spoken at the right time during a conversation; a letter to the editor; an offer of help to someone in need. We will find countless ways to take a stand if we have come to a clear conviction on right and wrong ourselves.

SPEED BUMP!

Slow down to be sure you have gotten the main points of this chapter.

Q1. What is the "kingdom stand" on race?

A1. The "kingdom stand" on race is that all people are created *equal* in the sight of God, and all discrimination is sin.

Q2. What is the "kingdom stand" on abortion?

A2. The "kingdom stand" on abortion is that human life is *sacred,* and the taking of innocent human life is a sin.

Q3. What is the "kingdom stand" on sexual purity?

A3. The "kingdom stand" on sexual purity is that sexual activity outside of *marriage* is sin.

Q4. What is the "kingdom stand" on fashion?

A4. The "kingdom stand" on fashion is that we are to dress or "appear" in a way that *honors* God.

Q5. What is the "kingdom stand" on entertainment?

A5. The "kingdom stand" on entertainment is that we will entertain ourselves only with those things that do not damage our progress toward *holiness.*

Q6. What is the "kingdom stand" on political involvement?

A6. The "kingdom stand" on political involvement is that Christians are obligated to *support* justice and righteousness in their political decisions.

Q7. What is the "kingdom stand" on the disadvantaged?

A7. The "kingdom stand" on the disadvantaged is that we ought to *help* those who cannot help themselves.

Q8. What is the "kingdom stand" on the church?

A8. The "kingdom stand" on the church is that the church is primarily in the *"righteousness"* business, and anytime another agenda supersedes that one, it has left its reason for existence.

Q9. What is the "kingdom stand" on evangelism?

A9. The "kingdom stand" on evangelism is that each Christian must accept personal responsibility for *involvement* in the Great Commission.

FILL IN THE BLANK

Q1. What is the "kingdom stand" on race?

A1. The "kingdom stand" on race is that all people are created _____ in the sight of God, and all discrimination is sin.

Q2. What is the "kingdom stand" on abortion?

A2. The "kingdom stand" on abortion is that human life is _____ , and the taking of innocent human life is a sin.

Q3. What is the "kingdom stand" on sexual purity?

A3. The "kingdom stand" on sexual purity is that sexual activity outside of _____ is sin.

Q4. What is the "kingdom stand" on fashion?

A4. The "kingdom stand" on fashion is that we are to dress or "appear" in a way that _____ God.

Q5. What is the "kingdom stand" on entertainment?

A5. The "kingdom stand" on entertainment is that we will entertain ourselves only with those things that do not damage our progress toward _____.

Q6. What is the "kingdom stand" on political involvement?

A6. The "kingdom stand" on political involvement is that Christians are obligated to _____ justice and righteousness in their political decisions.

Q7. What is the "kingdom stand" on the disadvantaged?

A7. The "kingdom stand" on the disadvantaged is that we ought to _____ those who cannot help themselves.

Q8. What is the "kingdom stand" on the church?

A8. The "kingdom stand" on the church is that the church is primarily in the " _____ " business, and anytime another agenda supersedes that one, it has left its reason for existence.

Q9. What is the "kingdom stand" on evangelism?

A9. The "kingdom stand" on evangelism is that each Christian must accept personal responsibility for _____ in the Great Commission.

FOR FURTHER THOUGHT AND DISCUSSION

1. How many of the above issues had you already come to a conviction about regarding right and wrong?

2. Are there any of the above that you disagree with? If you do, why?

3. What are the issues you believe are important and that you would add to the above list?

4. How faithful have you been to taking a stand on kingdom issues? What do you think you could/should do to be more faithful?

WHAT IF I DON'T BELIEVE?

If I don't believe in the importance of taking a stand on kingdom issues, I become part of the problem in the church rather than part of the solution. I become part of the "chameleon brigade" that blends in with the rest of society, even when it takes some occasional compromise to do it.

In doing so, I fail to honor God when it costs me something, I miss out on the rich blessings of being used by Him in important ways in people's lives, and I am not a good friend to my fellow man who may want desperately to hear what I have to say, but can't, because I don't say it.

FOR FURTHER STUDY

1. Scripture

- Matthew 12:26
- Matthew 22:21
- Mark 1:15
- Romans 14:17
- 1 Corinthians 16:13

2. Books

Several other books are very helpful in studying this subject further. They are listed below in general order of difficulty. If I could read only one of these, I would read the first one.

A Dangerous Grace, Charles Colson

Abortion and the Conscience of the Nation, Ronald Reagan (Abortion)

The Unaborted Socrates, Peter Kreeft (Abortion)

Making Choices, Peter Kreeft

Why Wait? What You Need to Know about the Teen Sexuality Crisis,
    Josh McDowell and Dick Day (Sexual Purity)

Life on the Edge, James Dobson (Sexual Purity)

12

WHAT IS THE FUTURE OF THE CHURCH?

At one time, the entire church on earth could be gotten into a large rowboat. Now look at it, with multiplied millions of members. What will it be like in heaven when everyone will be there!
—**Anonymous**

What is the future of the church? What will become of us? What will we be? What will we do? What will life be like?

We don't really know. The Bible gives us some glimpses, but we don't know how much of the glimpses to take literally and how much to take symbolically. For example, in the first chapter of Revelation we read a description of Jesus with white hair, glowing eyes, and powerful voice, yet He has a sword coming out of His mouth. Therefore, the sword must be symbolic. So is the whiteness symbolic too? What about the fire in the eyes? We are not sure what to make of heavenly descriptions.

Then, in chapter 21 we read of a heavenly city that has streets of gold, and yet the gold is transparent, so it is not the gold that we are familiar with on earth. Is the city symbolic? If so, why does the Lord then go to the trouble of giving the dimensions? Are the dimensions literal or symbolic?

Many good Bible teachers disagree on these matters. Even so, we can get to the heart of what heaven will be like for the church through some clear passages in Scripture. Relationships will be at the heart of our existence in heaven just as they are on earth, which should come as no surprise, since we are created in the image of God.

There is an amazing picture in Revelation 3:20–21 that gives us a glimpse of God's priorities for us.

> Behold, I stand at the door and knock. If anyone hears My voice and opens the door, I will come in to him and dine with him, and he with Me. To him who overcomes I will grant to sit with Me on My throne, as I also overcame and sat down with My Father on His throne.

Two things emerge from this passage. First, we will live in intimate fellowship with Jesus ("I will come in to him and dine with him"). The picture of dining in oriental culture is one of intimate fellowship. Meals, to them, were times of close hospitality and social interaction. Second, we will reign with Him over creation ("sit with Me on My throne"). The throne is a picture of power and authority.

WHAT WILL THE CHURCH BE IN HEAVEN?

The church will be the bride of Christ and will live in intimate personal relationship with one another and with God.

In Revelation 3:20, the picture of Jesus calling us to fellowship with Himself is an astonishing one. He is knocking on the door of our lives. He wants us to let Him in. He wants to dine with us, which means much more than filling His stomach while in the same room with us. We hardly know how to respond. We are like a tough street kid who has been abused and abandoned. We don't know how to act when a wealthy, emotionally healthy family adopts us and calls us their own. We have to get used to it. At first, we don't know how to respond to their affection and gestures of love. At first, we are standoffish. We don't even know what some of the gestures mean, let alone have the security to respond in kind. We react roughly and crudely because we don't know what else to do. At first when they tell us they love us, we don't reply. We act as though we didn't hear. Later when we have warmed up a bit, we say thanks. It is only after their love has warmed us and taught us that we can say, in return, "I love you too."

IN THIS CHAPTER WE LEARN THAT . . .

1. The church will be the bride of Christ and will live in intimate personal relationship with one another and with God.
2. The church will reign with Christ over creation for eternity.

And so it is with God's love. It is so overwhelming, so far beyond us, and we are so limited, so stunted in our capacity to give and receive love that we cannot yet even take in all the love God has given us and promises to give us.

The same image hit Peggy Noonan hard too. A former speechwriter for Presidents Ronald Reagan and George H. W. Bush, she wrote in *Life, Liberty and the Pursuit of Happiness* of her spiritual journey as an Irish Catholic back to her spiritual roots:

I got into a conversation with the man at the cash register [at the bookstore]. I don't recall what we were talking about, but I don't think it had anything to do with religion. But he picked up a book from a pile of books near the cash register and said, "You might be interested in this." It was called *Centering Prayer*, by Basil Pennington. So I took it home, and there, in the first few pages was the God of Revelation: "Look, I am standing at the door, knocking. If one of you hears me calling and opens the door, I will come in to share his meal, side by side with him." It *struck me hard: I had never thought of him at the door trying to get to me. I thought I was at the door trying to get to him* (emphasis added).

That phrase began to follow me. A week later, at Mass, the priest used as the central image in his homily a stained-glass window near the back of the church. In it, he noted, Christ is standing at a door, and waiting for those inside, us, to open it to him. "Take a look as you leave," he said, "you'll notice there is only one handle on the door, and it faces those inside the room. Only they can open it; Christ cannot. He waits; he is humble." (220)

I confess that my historic reaction had been the same as Ms. Noonan's. All the time, I thought I was at the door trying to get to Him. Here, He has been at the door trying to get to me. How amazing!

Would it be easier to understand the contrast if we imagined the queen of England knocking on the door of a scullery maid's house, wanting to come in and get to know her, to be friends with her? Or how about the president knocking on the door of an itinerant farm worker, seeking out his friendship? The scullery maid and the itinerant farm worker would be flabbergasted at the apparent reversal of hopes. What does a scullery maid have that the queen of England could want? What does an itinerant farm worker have that the president could want? What in the world do we have that God could want? Why in the world would Jesus be knocking on our door, and why in the world would we hesitate to open it?

Life is a mystery!

The picture of God's desire to be in close relationship with us is even more clear in the Scripture than just Revelation 3:20. That passage gives us the general picture of God's desire to be with us, but other passages are more specific. We are pictured as a bride and Jesus as the bridegroom. The fellowship God wants to have with us is not the camaraderie of good friends, but the intimacy, the oneness of husband and wife. In 2 Corinthians 11:2, we read, "For I am jealous for you with godly jealousy. For I have betrothed you to one husband, that I may present you as a chaste virgin to Christ." In Ephesians 5:25–27, we read,

Husbands, love your wives, just as Christ also loved the church and gave Himself for her, that He might sanctify and cleanse her with the washing of water by the word, that He might present her to Himself a glorious church, not having spot or wrinkle or any such thing, but that she should be holy and without blemish.

In Revelation 19:7–9, this picture of the church as the bride of Christ is furthered with the picture of the actual marriage ceremony:

Let us be glad and rejoice and give Him glory, for the marriage of the Lamb has come, and His wife has made herself ready. And to her it was granted to be arrayed in fine linen, clean and bright, for the fine linen is the righteous acts of the saints. Then he said to me, "Write: 'Blessed are those who are called to the marriage supper of the Lamb!'"

You have all been to weddings. They are wonderful affairs. The church is decorated splendidly with flowers and candles and ribbons, all testifying to the specialness of the occasion. The bride and groom are decked out in clothes so fine that many never wear such fine clothes again. All the family and friends are there.

> Imagine the president seeking out the friendship of a migrant farm worker. Yet Christ knocks on our door, seeking friendship with us.

And on whom is the primary focus? Not on the groom, but on the bride. As the ceremony begins, the groom steps in from the front, almost unnoticed. Then, beautifully attired ladies walk down the aisle in anticipation of the coming of the bride. A little girl follows, dropping rose petals on the floor to adorn the walkway for the coming of the bride. Finally the moment has come. There is a brief pause in the subdued music. Then, the volume is turned up and the organ blasts out the musical announcement: Here comes the bride! With surging strains from the ecstatic organ filling the sanctuary, all rise and turn to the back as the bride comes into view. The room murmurs at her radiance. She walks slowly, arm in arm with her father. The whole room turns slowly as she passes. Only when she arrives at the front does the ceremony begin.

Now, take this in.

In heaven, we are the bride. We are the focus of attention. We are the beautiful one. The holy halls will be filled with gasps of astonishment at our beauty as we come into view during the marriage of the Lamb. Joy reigns. And Jesus, our strong one, our handsome one, our eternal husband, is there, proudly waiting for the moment when we will be His forever, to become one eternally. The image of a marriage is not an accident. God created marriage in order to give us a picture of the relationship we will have with Jesus in heaven forever.

Why? Why would Jesus want to marry us? We think that is like Prince Charming wanting to marry Plain Jane, or the princess wanting to marry the frog. But we are wrong. We don't realize who we are, or we wouldn't think that. We are God's created and chosen ones, with inherent and infinite value, simply because we are created in His image.

WHY I NEED TO KNOW THIS

I need to know this so that I will understand that there is much to look forward to after I die.

Perhaps this analogy might capture the idea better. Suppose that in a faraway land, a beautiful daughter is born to a rich and powerful king and his lovely queen. The tiny infant is the joy of their lives. Yet one day, tragedy strikes. An evil kidnapper takes the child away and sells her in the slave market in another distant land. This daughter of a king grows up having no idea who she is, no idea that she has royal blood flowing through her veins, no idea that she is deeply and tenderly loved, no idea that she is wealthy and powerful and esteemed beyond imagination. As far as she knows, she is nothing but a worthless slave.

As she grows to adulthood, she could not know that the king has spared nothing in his search for her, but to no avail. One day, however, the prince of a neighboring country to the king's learns of the story of the beautiful princess and vows to find her. Facing hardship, deprivation, and threat to life, he finally locates the princess, tells her who she is, and asks her to marry him.

The princess cannot take it in. She knows herself only as a lowly slave. She is willing to believe that she is a princess, but even then, it is hard, and she cannot imagine what it means. She doesn't feel rich. She doesn't feel powerful. She doesn't feel like royalty. She has to take it all by faith. But the day comes when they arrive back home to the fanfare of two nations. There is music, laughter, and shouts of joy. Two entire nations look on as in regal splendor the two are married, move into one palace, and live happily ever after. Only as the princess begins to experience reality can she grasp reality.

Perhaps that pictures who we really are, but why we have trouble grasping it. Perhaps that will help us catch a glimpse of why Jesus would want to marry us. We are children of a king, being restored to Him, even though we may not feel like it yet.

WHAT WILL THE CHURCH DO IN HEAVEN?

The church will reign with Christ over creation for eternity.

Fellowship is not the only thing we will have in heaven. We will also have plenty to do. Therefore, the image of a bride and marriage is not the only "picture" that we have to understand our life there. In addition to being the bride of Christ, we are also the brother of Christ (Romans 8:29). We are joint heirs with Him (Romans 8:17). What He has, we'll have. What He rules, we'll rule. His inheritance will be our inheritance.

It seems almost blasphemous to call Christ our brother, and I wouldn't have the nerve to do it if I didn't read it in Scripture. And it seems almost blasphemous to suggest that we will be joint heirs with Him, that what He owns, we'll own. The only way I have the nerve to do it is that Scripture calls us joint heirs.

But I want to make something else clear. We will not be on an even plane with Jesus. He is still our God and our King. He is still the Lord whom we worship and serve. We will still spend eternity praising and thanking and worshiping Him for the gift of redemption. He will not be our heavenly buddy. We will not put our arm around His shoulder and stroll off into the celestial meadows for an eternity of play. He is still God and we are still His created ones. But, we will still be His spiritual brother and we will still rule and reign with Him over all creation for all time.

What all this involves, we don't know. It will involve judging angels. First Corinthians 6:3 says, "Do you not know that we shall judge angels? How much more, things that pertain to this life?" Perhaps new things will be created for us to rule over. Perhaps we will each be given a galaxy to rule over, to make as special and beautiful as we can, and then give it back to God as a gift to Him.

And the reign will never come to an end. Revelation 22:4–5 says, "They [the redeemed] shall see His face, and His name shall be on their foreheads. There shall be no night there: They need no lamp nor light of the sun, for the Lord God gives them light. And they shall reign forever and ever."

There is not a great deal of information in the Bible about what we will actually do in heaven. Perhaps it is because it would be too hard for us to understand this side of heaven.

It would be like trying to describe modern technology and civilization to a Stone Age tribe in the Philippines. They simply couldn't grasp "Los Angeles," the information superhighway, or subatomic medical research.

As helpless as we would be at understanding modern civilization if we were living on a Stone Age level, we are even more helpless in trying to fully envision heaven and what we will do there. The Bible has told us that:

- The focus will be on meaningful relationships, with God and with one another.
- We will reign with Christ.
- It will be beautiful.
- It will be free of all sin, death, and pain.

In addition, since we are created in the image of God, and if this world gives us any glimpses of heaven, we can imagine several other things:

- We will love to create.
- There will be lots of fun.
- We will work hard.
- There will be no end, either in size or time.

In addition to fellowship and worship, the church will have plenty to do in heaven.

CONCLUSION

In *Growing In Christ*, James Packer described at significant length the meaning of the Apostles' Creed. He ends his study by saying,

> I have been writing with enthusiasm, for this everlasting life is something to which I look forward. Why? Not because I am out of love with life here—just the reverse! My life is full of joy, from four sources—knowing God, and people, and the good and pleasant things that God and men under God have created, and doing things which are worthwhile for God or others, or for myself as God's man. But my reach exceeds my grasp. My relationships with God and others are never as rich and full as I want them to be, and I am always finding more than I thought was there in great music, great verse, great books, great lives, and the great kaleidoscope of the natural order.
>
> As I get older, I find that I appreciate God, and people, and good and lovely and noble things, more and more intensely; so it is pure delight to think that this enjoyment will continue and increase in some form (what form, God knows, and I am content to wait and see), literally forever. Christians inherit in fact the destiny which

fairy tales envisage in fancy: *we* (yes, you and I, the silly saved sinners) live, and live *happily,* and by God's endless mercy will live happily *ever after.* (88–89)

SPEED BUMP!

Slow down to be sure you have gotten the main points of this chapter.

Q1. What will the church be in heaven?

A1. The church will be the bride of Christ and will live in intimate personal *relationship* with one another and with God.

Q2. What will the church do in heaven?

A2. The church will *reign* with Christ over creation for eternity.

FILL IN THE BLANK

Q1. What will the church be in heaven?

A1. The church will be the bride of Christ and will live in intimate personal _____ with one another and with God.

Q2. What will the church do in heaven?

A2. The church will _____ with Christ over creation for eternity.

FOR FURTHER THOUGHT AND DISCUSSION

1. What is the most satisfying interpersonal relationship you have or have had on earth? What makes or made it so satisfying? Factoring in the concept of "perfection," what do you think will be the characteristics of relationships with God and other Christians in heaven?

2. What is it about heaven that holds the greatest attraction for you?

3. What do you like to do more than anything else on earth? Do you think that what you enjoy will exist, in principle, in heaven?

WHAT IF I DON'T BELIEVE?

If I don't believe in the future of the church, I have very little to look forward to after death. I may find it more difficult to give up or miss out on things in this life if I think this life is all there is. If I have the hope of a rewarding existence in heaven, I may be better able to sacrifice desires in this life and endure the unavoidable pain of this life.

FOR FURTHER STUDY

1. Scripture

- Romans 8:17
- 2 Corinthians 11:2
- Ephesians 5:25–27
- Revelation 1:12–16
- Revelation 3:20
- Revelation 19:7–9
- Revelation 21:9–22:5

2. Books

Other books can be helpful in studying this subject further. If I could read only one of these, I would read the first one.

Eternity, Joseph Stowell

Heaven Help Us! Steven Lawson

BIBLIOGRAPHY

Colson, Charles. *Faith on the Line.* Wheaton, IL: Victor Books, 1994.

_____. *The Body.* Dallas: Word Publishing, 1992.

Getz, Gene. *The Measure of a Man.* Ventura, CA: Regal Books, 1995.

Green, Michael. *Baptism.* Downers Grove, IL: InterVarsity Press, 1987.

Jacobsen, Marion. *Saints and Snobs.* Wheaton, IL: Tyndale House, 1972.

Kushner, Harold. *Who Needs God?* New York: Summit Books, 1989.

Noonan, Peggy. *Life, Liberty and the Pursuit of Happiness.* Holbrook, MA: Adams Publishing, 1994.

Packer, James I. *Concise Theology.* Wheaton, IL: Tyndale House, 1993.

_____. *Growing in Christ.* Wheaton, IL: Chosen Books, 1994.

Shelley, Bruce. *The Church.* Wheaton, IL: Victor Books, 1978.

_____. *Why Baptism?* Downers Grove, IL: InterVarsity Press, 1987.

Sproul, R. C. *Essential Truths of the Christian Faith.* Wheaton, IL: Tyndale House, 1992.

Swindoll, Charles. *The Bride.* Grand Rapids: Zondervan, 1994.

ten Boom, Corrie. *Tramp for the Lord.* Fort Washington, PA: Christian Literature Crusade, Inc., 1974.

Wiersbe, Warren. *The Biblical Exposition Commentary,* Vol. 1. Wheaton, IL: Victor Books, 1989.

_____. *The Integrity Crisis.* Nashville: Oliver-Nelson Books, 1988.

MASTER REVIEW

Chapter 1

Q1. What is the universal church?

A1. The universal church is made up of all true *Christians* everywhere, past, present, and future.

Q2. How is the universal church pictured in Scripture?

A2. The universal church is pictured in Scripture by a *body,* a building, and a bride.

Q3. What is the local church?

A3. A local church is a group of believers who agree together to pursue the *ideals* of the universal church.

Chapter 2

Q1. What is the Apostles' Creed?

A1. The Apostles' Creed is an ancient statement of the *essentials* of the Christian faith.

Q2. Who is God the Father?

A2. God the Father is the sovereign *Creator* of the universe.

Q3. Who is Jesus?

A3. Jesus of Nazareth is the Son of God and *Savior* of humanity.

Q4. Who is the Holy Spirit?

A4. The Holy Spirit is God, the third member of the Trinity, and helper of all Christians.

Q5. What is the universal church?

A5. The universal church is the totality of all *believers* in Jesus from all places and all times.

Q6. What is personal salvation?

A6. Personal salvation is the experience by which a person by grace through faith in Jesus *is forgiven* of sins and given eternal life.

Chapter 3

Q1. What is faith?

A1. Faith is believing what God has said and *acting* accordingly.

Q2. What is hope?

A2. Hope is putting your confidence in the *future*.

Q3. What is love?

A3. Love is the exercise of my *will* for the good of another.

Chapter 4

Q1. Why should the church worship?

A1. The church should worship because we are *instructed* to worship and because the *example* of the early church teaches us to worship.

Q2. What does it mean to worship?

A2. To worship means to *prostrate* oneself before God.

Q3. How should we worship?

A3. We should worship in a way that is culturally *relevant* without violating any principle in Scripture.

Q4. Who is the audience in worship?

A4. Worshipers are the "actors" in worship and *God* is the audience.

Q5. What should our focus be in worship?

A5. Our worship should include a *dual* focus on the greatness and the nearness of God.

Chapter 5

Q1. Why should the church teach the Scriptures?

A1. The church should teach the Scriptures to help people master the Bible well enough to *mature* spiritually.

Q2. Why should the church promote fellowship?

A2. The church should promote fellowship because Christians need each other for *support* to live the Christian life.

Q3. Why must the church minister to others?

A3. The church must minister because of the *needs* of Christians within the church as well as the needs of those outside the church.

Chapter 6

Q1. What are the biblical positions of church leadership?

A1. The Bible mentions pastor-teachers, elders, and deacons as the *three* leadership ministries of the church.

Q2. What is the basis of leadership in the church?

A2. The basis of leadership in the church is *spiritual* maturity.

Chapter 7

Q1. What does it mean to be above reproach?

A1. To be above reproach means that you have a *good reputation* because you have no major character faults.

Q2. What does it mean to be the husband of one wife?

A2. To be the husband of one wife means, at least, that a husband *is faithful* to his wife in thought, word, and deed.

Q3. What does it mean to be temperate?

A3. To be temperate means to be self-controlled and *moderate* in attitude and actions.

Q4. What does it mean to be prudent?

A4. To be prudent means to be *skilled* in managing practical affairs.

Q5. What does it mean to be respectable?

A5. To be respectable means to be *proper* in behavior.

Q6. What does it mean to be hospitable?

A6. To be hospitable means to be *kind* to strangers.

Q7. What does it mean to be able to teach?

A7. To be able to teach means that by virtue of one's life, one's knowledge, and one's ability to communicate, he is *qualified* to teach others.

Q8. What does it mean to not be addicted to wine?

A8. Not addicted to wine means not drinking alcoholic beverages habitually or *compulsively.*

Q9. What does it mean to not be self-willed?

A9. Not self-willed means that you do not *demand* your own way.

Q10. What does it mean to not be quick-tempered?

A10. Not quick-tempered means that you *control* your anger and only express anger at the things that anger God.

Q11. What does it mean not to be pugnacious?

A11. Not to be pugnacious means that you are not a *fighter,* either verbally or physically.

Q12. What does it mean to be gentle?

A12. To be gentle means to treat with *care,* so as to soothe and not to hurt.

Q13. What does it mean to be uncontentious?

A13. To be uncontentious means that you are not quarrelsome or *argumentative.*

Q14. What does it mean to be free from the love of money?

A14. To be free from the love of money means that you do not *want* money more than you want the will of God.

Q15. What does it mean to manage one's household well?

A15. To manage one's household well means to *lead* one's family with care and diligence.

Q16. What does it mean not to be a new convert?

A16. Not to be a new convert means that sufficient *time* has passed since becoming a Christian.

Q17. What does it mean to love what is good?

A17. To love what is good means that we *choose* to do good rather than evil.

Q18. What does it mean to be just?

A18. To be just means to give *equal* weight to all people and actions.

Q19. What does it mean to be devout?

A19. To be devout means to earnestly *pursue* one's faith.

Q20. What does it mean to be self-controlled?

A20. To be self-controlled means to be personally *disciplined* in all things.

Chapter 8

Q1. What is baptism?

A1. Baptism is a symbolic act in which Christians *proclaim* their belief in Jesus' death and resurrection.

Q2. What happens when we are baptized?

A2. There are *three* views as to what happens when we are baptized: the Catholic view, the Covenant view, and the Baptist view.

Q3. Who is baptized?

A3. While there are responsible *differences* of perspective, everyone believes that all adult believers should be baptized, and some believe that all children of Christians should be baptized.

Q4. How are we to baptize?

A4. There are *three* forms of baptism: sprinkling, pouring, and immersion.

Q5. What is the Lord's Supper?

A5. The Lord's Supper is a ceremonial meal of bread and the fruit of the vine *commemorating* the death of Jesus for our sins, and celebrating His new covenant with us.

Chapter 9

Q1. What is episcopalian government?

A1. Episcopalian government is a *hierarchical* system of governing and decision-making in the church in which denominational leaders are the primary authority.

Q2. What is presbyterian government?

A2. Presbyterian government is a *representative* system of governing and decision-making in the church in which a board of elders is the primary authority.

Q3. What is congregational government?

A3. Congregational government is a *democratic* system of governing and decision-making in the church in which the congregation as a whole is the primary authority.

Chapter 10

Q1. Why do individuals need the church?

A1. Individuals need the church to help them be successful in their *personal* lives.

Q2. Why does the church need individuals?

A2. The church needs individuals to help it be successful in its *corporate* life.

Chapter 11

Q1. What is the "kingdom stand" on race?

A1. The "kingdom stand" on race is that all people are created *equal* in the sight of God, and all discrimination is sin.

Q2. What is the "kingdom stand" on abortion?

A2. The "kingdom stand" on abortion is that human life is *sacred,* and the taking of innocent human life is a sin.

Q3. What is the "kingdom stand" on sexual purity?

A3. The "kingdom stand" on sexual purity is that sexual activity outside of *marriage* is sin.

Q4. What is the "kingdom stand" on fashion?

A4. The "kingdom stand" on fashion is that we are to dress or "appear" in a way that *honors* God.

Q5. What is the "kingdom stand" on entertainment?

A5. The "kingdom stand" on entertainment is that we will entertain ourselves only with those things that do not damage our progress toward *holiness*.

Q6. What is the "kingdom stand" on political involvement?

A6. The "kingdom stand" on political involvement is that Christians are obligated to *support* justice and righteousness in their political decisions.

Q7. What is the "kingdom stand" on the disadvantaged?

A7. The "kingdom stand" on the disadvantaged is that we ought to *help* those who cannot help themselves.

Q8. What is the "kingdom stand" on the church?

A8. The "kingdom stand" on the church is that the church is primarily in the "*righteousness*" business, and anytime another agenda supersedes that one, it has left its reason for existence.

Q9. What is the "kingdom stand" on evangelism?

A9. The "kingdom stand" on evangelism is that each Christian must accept personal responsibility for *involvement* in the Great Commission.

Chapter 12

Q1. What will the church be in heaven?

A1. The church will be the bride of Christ and will live in intimate personal *relationship* with one another and with God.

Q2. What will the church do in heaven?

A2. The church will *reign* with Christ over creation for eternity.

ABOUT THE AUTHOR

Max Anders (Th.M. Dallas Theological Seminary, D. Min Western Seminary) is the author of over 20 books and the creator and general editor of the thirty-two volume Holman Bible Commentary. Dr. Anders has taught on the college and seminary level, was one of the original team members with Walk Thru the Bible Ministries, and has pastored for over 20 years. He is the founder and president of 7 Marks, Inc., a ministry specializing in discipleship strategies and materials for local churches (www.7marks.org). His book *30 Days to Understanding the Bible* has reached more than 300,000 readers with a passion for learning God's Word.

Printed in the USA
CPSIA information can be obtained
at www.ICGtesting.com
JSHW030059260324
59867JS00008B/64

9 781418 548568